from the staff

Discover the time-honored tradition of appliqué with this collection of heirloom quality quilts. While each appliqué is stitched completely by hand, all the projects utilize a variety of techniques for preparing the pieces for appliqué.

With the step-by-step instructions in the Appliqué Primer and basic quiltmaking techniques in Quilting Basics, you'll find all the information you'll need to successfully complete your hand-appliqué projects. If you're a beginner, our easy-to-follow photos will give you the confidence to try new techniques. If you're an experienced quilter, you'll discover here a valuable reference for reviewing and brushing up on techniques.

Whatever your skill level, you'll find a quilting project to fit any season or gift-giving occasion. Re-create the projects exactly as shown—or create your own unique color palette to fit your décor or tastes. Our hope is that you'll be pleased with the results and will find that hand appliqué is a skill you'll put to use frequently as you progress on your quilting journey.

enjoy!

table of contents

12

40

58

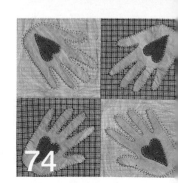

68

74

traditional
appliqué

Embark on your hand-appliqué journey with this collection of quilts, perfect for honing your stitching skills. Once you've mastered the basic stitch, try your hand at other traditional methods including needle-turn and double-appliqué.

dutch
blue

Inspired by traditional folk art paper-cuttings, this design involves cutting the motif from a folded piece of fabric before appliquéing it to the background.

Designer: Bettina Havig   Photographer: Perry Struse

materials

¾ yard of indigo blue tone-on-tone print for cutwork appliqué and inner border

¾ yard of light blue print for appliqué foundation and inner border

⅞ yard of blue print for outer border and binding

1⅛ yard of backing fabric

38" square of quilt batting

Freezer paper

FINISHED QUILT TOP: 32" square

Quantities specified for 44/45"-wide, 100% cotton fabrics. All measurements include a ¼" seam allowance. Sew with right sides together unless otherwise stated.

cut the fabrics

To make the best use of your fabrics, cut the pieces in the order that follows. The patterns are on *page 6*. To make templates of the patterns, follow the instructions in Appliqué Primer, which begins on *page 84*.

From indigo blue tone-on-tone print, cut:
- 1—20" square for cutwork appliqué
- 22—2⅞" squares, cutting each in half diagonally for a total of 44 triangles, *or* 44 of Triangle Pattern

From light blue print, cut:
- 1—22" square for appliqué foundation
- 22—2⅞" squares, cutting each in half diagonally for a total of 44 triangles, *or* 44 of Triangle Pattern

From blue print, cut:
- 4—2×42" binding strips
- 4—4½×32½" outer border strips

From freezer paper, cut:
- 1—18" square

appliqué the cutwork design

1. Fold the freezer paper 18" square in half horizontally, making a rectangle (see Diagram 1). Fold the rectangle in half, making a 9" square. Then fold the square in half diagonally, bringing together the folded edges. Staple the folds together in a corner to keep them stable.

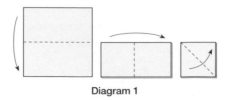

Diagram 1

2. Position the Heart Cutwork Pattern on the folded freezer paper as indicated. Tape or glue the pattern securely to the folded freezer paper. (Designer Bettina Havig uses a dry-mount adhesive because it allows the pattern to be removed and reused.)

3. Strategically pin or staple the layers to keep them from moving while cutting. Cut out the design on the solid traced lines, including the inside open areas, to make a freezer-paper template. Remove the pins or staples.

4. Carefully unfold the freezer paper. Position the freezer paper shiny side down on the right side of the indigo blue tone-on-tone print 20" square. Using a dry iron on the cotton setting, press the freezer paper onto the indigo fabric. Trace the outline of the cutwork design with a light-color fabric marker. You will need to see these marks throughout the appliqué process. Be sure that every part of the design has been traced; then remove the freezer paper.

5. Match the center of the marked indigo blue square to the center of the light blue print 22" square foundation, aligning the fabrics' straight edges. Baste through the center of the drawn heart cutwork pattern. The basting should hold the design in place until appliquéing is complete and should not be in the way of your needle-turn stitching.

6. Cut out a small portion of the appliqué design (about ⅛ to ⅙"), cutting a scant ⅛" away from the drawn lines so the lines can be your turn-under guide. Be careful not to cut the foundation fabric. Snip deeply only inside the curves, and then sparingly. By cutting a little at a time, the piece remains more stable. Appliqué the portion in place with small blind stitches, turning the edges under with your needle as you work.

When appliquéing is complete, trim the light blue print foundation to measure 20½" square, including the seam allowances, being sure to center the cutwork design.

assemble and add the inner border

1. Sew together one light blue print triangle and one indigo blue tone-on-tone print triangle to make a triangle-square (see Diagram 2). Press the seam allowance toward the indigo blue print triangle. The pieced triangle-square should measure 2½" square, including the seam allowances. Repeat to make a total of 44 triangle-squares.

Diagram 2

2. Referring to the photograph *opposite* for placement, join 10 triangle-squares in a horizontal row to make an inner border strip. Press the seam allowances in one direction. Repeat to make a second inner border strip. Sew the inner border strips to opposite edges of the appliquéd quilt center. Press the seam allowances toward the appliquéd square.

3. Sew together 12 triangle-squares in a vertical row to make an inner border strip. Press the seam allowances in one direction. Repeat to make a second inner border strip. Sew the inner border strips to the remaining edges of the appliquéd square to complete the quilt center. Press the seam allowances toward the appliquéd square. The pieced quilt center should measure 24½" square, including the seam allowances.

add the outer border

1. With midpoints aligned, pin a blue print 4½×32½" outer border strip to each edge of the pieced quilt center; allow excess border fabric to extend beyond the edges. Sew each border strip to the quilt center, beginning and ending the seams ¼" from the corners (see Diagram 3). Press the seam allowances toward the border strips.

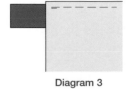

Diagram 3

2. To miter a border corner, overlap the border strips. Align the edge of a right triangle with the raw edge of the border strip on top so the long edge of the triangle intersects the seam in the corner (see Diagram 4). With a pencil, draw along the edge of the triangle from the seam out to the raw edge. Place the bottom border strip on top and repeat the marking process.

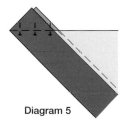

Diagram 4

3. Match the marked lines and pin (see Diagram 5).

Diagram 5

4. Beginning with a backstitch at the inside corner, stitch exactly on the marked lines to the raw edges of the border strips. Check the right side of the corner to see that it lies flat. Then trim the excess fabric, leaving a ¼" seam allowance. Press the seam open.

5. Miter the remaining corners in the same manner to complete the quilt top.

complete the quilt

1. Layer the quilt top, batting, and backing according to the instructions in Quilting Basics, which begins on *page 94*.

2. Quilt as desired. Bettina hand-quilted around the appliquéd cutwork design, echoing the design with at least three lines spaced about ½" apart.

3. Use the blue print 2×42" strips to bind the quilt according to the instructions in Quilting Basics.

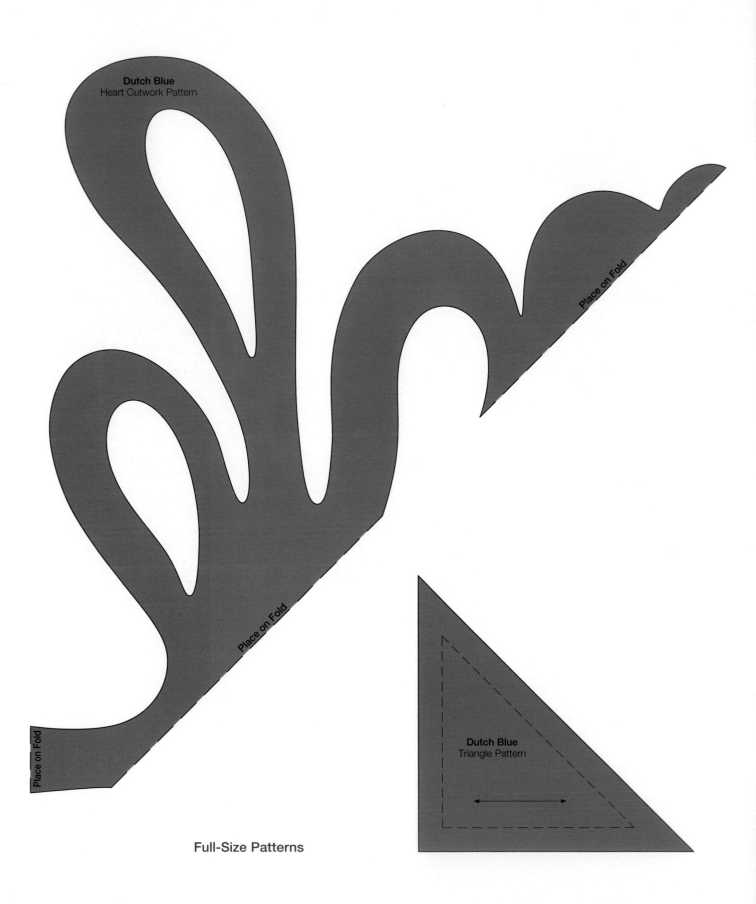

Dutch Blue
Heart Cutwork Pattern

Place on Fold

Place on Fold

Place on Fold

Dutch Blue
Triangle Pattern

Full-Size Patterns

sweet lullabies

A perfect beginner project, this delightful appliqué album quilt was inspired by a vintage baby quilt from the 1850s.

Designer: Peggy Kotek   Photographer: Perry Struse

materials

1⅝ yards of cream print for appliqué foundations, sashing, borders, and binding
⅓ yard of pink print for appliqués
⅛ yard of solid pink for appliqués
½ yard of solid green for appliqués and sawtooth border
Scrap of light green print for appliqués
1⅛ yards of backing fabric
41" square of quilt batting
Embroidery floss: green
Freezer paper

FINISHED QUILT TOP: 35" square
FINISHED BLOCK: 10" square

Quantities specified for 44/45"-wide, 100% cotton fabrics. All measurements include a ¼" seam allowance. Sew with right sides together unless otherwise stated.

cut the fabrics

To make the best use of your fabrics, cut the pieces in the order that follows. The patterns begin on *page 10.* To make templates of the patterns, follow the instructions in the Appliqué Primer, which begins on *page 84.* For Pattern H, follow steps 1 and 2 under Cut and Appliqué the Fleur-de-Lis Block on *page 9* to trace a complete template.

To use the freezer-paper appliqué method, as was used in this project, complete the following steps.

1. Position the freezer paper, shiny side down, over all patterns except H. With a pencil, trace each pattern the number of times indicated. Cut out the freezer-paper templates on the traced lines.

2. Press the freezer-paper templates onto the right sides of the designated fabrics; let cool.

3. Cut out the fabric shapes, adding a ³⁄₁₆" seam allowance. Remove the template and reuse.

From cream print, cut:
- 4—2×42" binding strips
- 2—4½×35½" outer border strips
- 2—4½×27½" outer border strips
- 2—2×24½" inner border strips
- 2—2×21½" inner border strips

- 1—1½×21½" sashing strip
- 4—10½" squares for appliqué foundations
- 2—1½×10½" sashing strips
- 33—2⅜" squares, cutting each in half diagonally for a total of 66 triangles
- 2—2" squares for sawtooth border

From pink print, cut:
- 1—10½" square for Pattern H
- 4 of Pattern A

From solid pink, cut:
- 13 of Pattern G
- 1 of Pattern J

From solid green, cut:
- 33—2⅜" squares, cutting each in half diagonally for a total of 66 triangles
- 12 of Pattern C
- 4 *each* of patterns D and I
- 1 of Pattern E
- 10 of Pattern F

From light green print, cut:
- 4 of Pattern B
- 1 of Pattern K

appliqué the rose block

1. Referring to the Rose Block Appliqué Placement Diagram, arrange the four pink print A roses, the four light green print B rose centers, the 12 solid green C leaves, and the four solid green D stems on a cream print 10½" square appliqué foundation. Baste in place.

Rose Block Appliqué Placement Diagram

2. Using green thread, appliqué the leaves to the foundation, starting each one at a stem's edge so all leaves touch a stem. Appliqué the remaining pieces in place using matching threads.

appliqué the cherry wreath block

1. To make templates for the cherries, trace Pattern G 13 times on lightweight card stock; cut out. Baste around the edge of each solid pink G cherry and gather each one around a card-stock template; press. When cool, cut threads and remove the templates.

2. Referring to the Cherry Wreath Block Appliqué Placement Diagram, arrange the solid green E ring, the 10 solid green F leaves, and the 13 solid pink G cherries on a cream print 10½" square appliqué foundation. Baste in place.

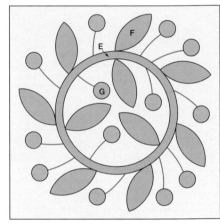

Cherry Wreath Block Appliqué Placement Diagram

3. Clip the inside edge of the seam allowance of the solid green E ring; using green thread, appliqué the ring to the foundation, sewing the inside edge first.

4. Using green thread, appliqué the leaves to the foundation, starting each one at the ring's edge so all leaves touch the ring.

5. Using two strands of green embroidery floss, stem-stitch the 13 cherry stems. (For specific instructions on stem stitching, see Embroidery Stitches on *page 93.*)

6. Appliqué each cherry to the foundation.

appliqué the leaf block

1. Referring to the Leaf Block Appliqué Placement Diagram, arrange the four solid green I leaves, the solid pink J bud, and the light green print K bud center on a cream print 10 1/2" square appliqué foundation. Baste in place.

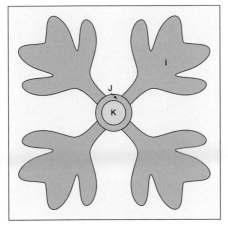

**Leaf Block Appliqué
Placement Diagram**

2. Using threads that match the fabrics, appliqué the pieces to the foundation.

cut and appliqué the fleur-de-lis block

Designer Peggy Kotek used freezer paper and needle-turn appliqué to create this block. The pattern piece is cut out as it is appliquéd to the foundation. The steps are as follows.

1. Cut a 10 1/2" square of freezer paper. Fold the freezer-paper square in half horizontally with the shiny side inside, then fold it in half again vertically; crease the folds.

2. Unfold the freezer paper and align adjacent horizontal and vertical crease lines with the dashed lines on Pattern H (Quarter Pattern); trace Pattern H. Refold the freezer paper. Strategically pin or staple the layers to keep them from moving while cutting. Cut out the design on the solid traced lines, including the center area, to make a freezer-paper template. Remove the pins or staples.

3. Carefully unfold the freezer-paper template and center it, shiny side down, on the right side of the pink print 10 1/2" square. Using a dry iron on the cotton setting, press the freezer paper onto the fabric. Trace the outline of the template with a light color fabric marker. (You will need to see these marks throughout the appliqué process.) Be sure that every part of the design has been traced; then remove the freezer paper.

4. Place the marked pink print square on the remaining cream print 10 1/2" square appliqué foundation, aligning the fabrics' straight edges. Baste the squares together. The basting should hold the design in place until appliquéing is complete and should not be in the way of your needle-turn stitching.

5. Cut out a small portion of the appliqué design at a time (about 1"), cutting a scant 3/16" away from the drawn lines so the lines can be your turn-under guide. Be careful not to cut the foundation fabric. Snip deeply only inside the curves, and then sparingly. By cutting a little at a time, the piece remains more stable. Appliqué the portion in place with small blind stitches and pink thread, turning the edge under with your needle as you work. Continue in the same manner until the entire fleur-de-lis is appliquéd to the foundation.

assemble the quilt center

1. Referring to the photograph on *page 7* for placement, lay out the four appliquéd blocks, the two cream print 1 1/2×10 1/2" sashing strips, and the cream print 1 1/2×21 1/2" sashing strip in horizontal rows.

2. Sew together the pieces in each row. Press the seam allowances toward the sashing strips. Join the rows to make the quilt center; press. The pieced quilt center should measure 21 1/2" square, including the seam allowances.

add the borders

1. Sew the cream print 2×21 1/2" inner border strips to opposite edges of the pieced quilt center. Add the cream print 2×24 1/2" inner border strips to the remaining edges of the pieced quilt center. Press the seam allowances toward the inner border.

2. Sew together one cream print triangle and one solid green triangle to make a triangle-square (see Triangle-Square Diagram, *above right*). Press the seam allowance toward the green triangle. The triangle-square should measure 2 3/8" square, including the seam allowances. Repeat to make a total of 66 triangle-squares.

Triangle-Square Diagram

3. Referring to the photograph on *page 7* for placement, sew together 16 triangle-squares to make a short sawtooth border unit; press. Repeat to make a second short sawtooth border unit. Sew the border units to opposite edges of the pieced quilt center. Press the seam allowances toward the cream print inner border.

4. Sew together 7 triangle-squares and one cream print 2 3/8" square to make a long sawtooth border unit; press. Repeat to make a second long sawtooth border unit. Join the units to the remaining edges of the pieced quilt center. Press the seam allowances toward the inner border.

5. Sew the cream print 4 1/2×27 1/2" outer border strips to opposite edges of the pieced quilt center. Then add the cream print 4 1/2×35 1/2" outer border strips to the remaining edges of the pieced quilt center to complete the quilt top. Press all seam allowances toward the outer border.

complete the quilt

1. Layer the quilt top, batting, and backing according to the instructions in Quilting Basics, which begins on *page 94*.

2. Quilt as desired. Peggy hand-quilted around each appliqué motif, then filled the background with diagonal stitching.

3. Use the cream print 2×42" strips to bind the quilt according to the instructions in Quilting Basics.

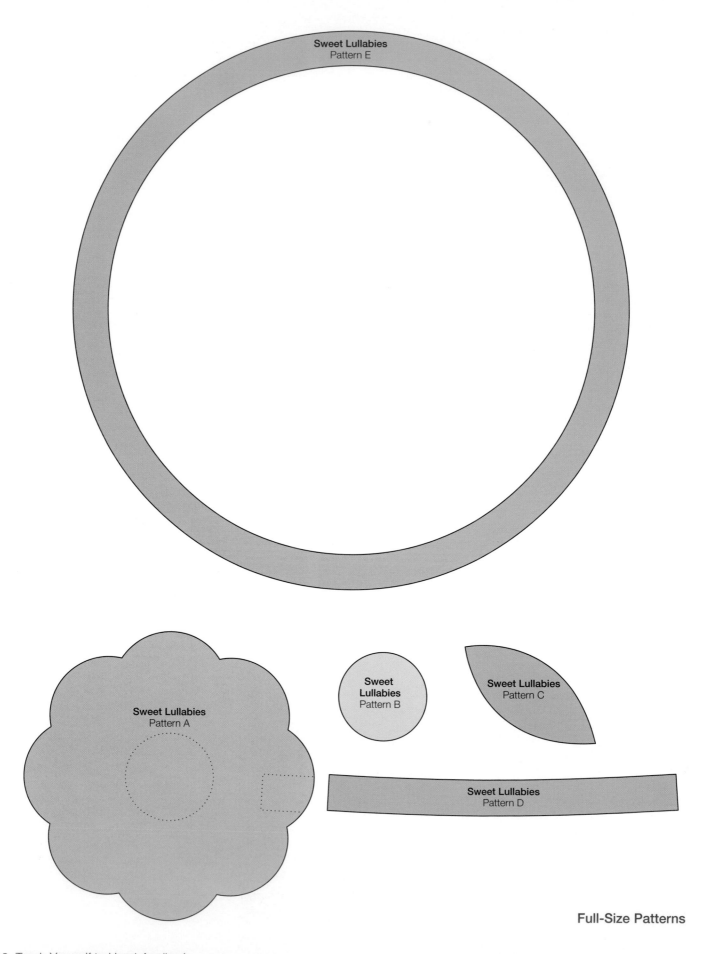

Sweet Lullabies
Pattern E

Sweet Lullabies
Pattern A

Sweet Lullabies
Pattern B

Sweet Lullabies
Pattern C

Sweet Lullabies
Pattern D

Full-Size Patterns

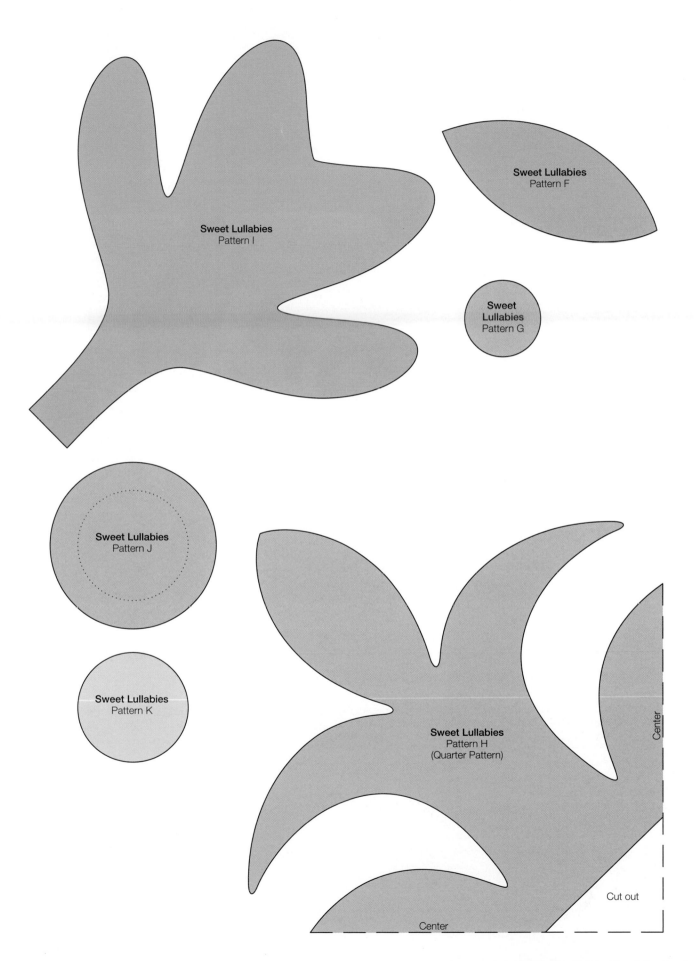

Sweet Lullabies
Pattern F

Sweet Lullabies
Pattern I

Sweet
Lullabies
Pattern G

Sweet Lullabies
Pattern J

Sweet Lullabies
Pattern K

Sweet Lullabies
Pattern H
(Quarter Pattern)

Center

Cut out

Center

i can fly

Delight in this whimsical folk art angel
who comes alive in easy double appliqué.
A pieced border of twirling pinwheels
adds to the quilt's breezy attitude.

Designer: Miriam Gourley   Photographer: Scott Little

materials

½ yard of antique gold print for appliqué foundation

18×22" piece (fat quarter) of tomato red print for star blocks

18×22" piece (fat quarter) of terra-cotta print for star blocks

18×22" piece (fat quarter) of dark cream print for star blocks

¼ yard of taupe print for checkerboard border

¼ yard of cream print for checkerboard border

¼ yard of purple print for sashing

⅝ yard of black plaid for borders and binding

Scraps of the following for appliqués:
   solid off-white for face and hands,
   dark brown print for hair,
   black check for legs,
   gold print for sleeves and dress,
   lavender print for wing,
   tomato red print for dress,
   solid black for pinwheel handle,
   rust and gold prints for yo-yos,
   solid green for pinwheel, and
   green print for pinwheel

1 yard of backing fabric

40×36" of thin cotton batting

Gold thread

Embroidery floss: dark brown, terra-cotta, and tan

½"-diameter terra-cotta button

Small, round stencil brush

Pink acrylic paint for cheek color

FINISHED QUILT TOP: 34×30"

Quantities specified for 44/45"-wide, 100% cotton fabrics. All measurements include a ¼" seam allowance. Sew with right sides together unless otherwise stated.

basic appliqué instructions

Designer Miriam Gourley saves time and creates smoother curves with her appliqué method: "I pin my template to a doubled piece of fabric. Then I put it in the sewing machine and stitch around the outside edge of the template. I cut a slit in the top layer only. As you turn it right side out, you'll have the exact shape." The following instructions describe her method.

1. Layer two pieces of the same fabric with right sides together. Pin a template to the doubled fabric piece.

2. Machine-stitch around the edge of the template (see Diagram 1). Avoid piercing the template with your needle.

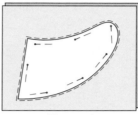

Diagram 1

3. Remove the template. Trim around the stitching, leaving an ⅛" seam allowance. Clip any angles or curves, but take care not to clip the stitching.

4. Carefully make a slit in the top layer of fabric where the template rested (see Diagram 2).

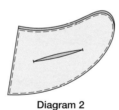

Diagram 2

5. Turn the appliqué piece right side out, and use a tool to push out any corners or angles. Press the piece.

cut the fabrics

To make the best use of your fabrics, cut the pieces in the order that follows.

The patterns begin on *page 15*. To make templates, follow the instructions in Appliqué Primer, which begins on *page 84*. Cut out the appliqué pieces following the Basic Appliqué Instructions at left.

From antique gold print, cut:
● 1—24×16" rectangle for appliqué foundation

From tomato red print, cut:
● 12—2⅞" squares, cutting each in half diagonally for a total of 24 triangles
● 6—2½" squares

From terra-cotta print, cut:
● 24—2½" squares

From dark cream print, cut:
● 12—2⅞" squares, cutting each in half diagonally for a total of 24 triangles

From taupe print, cut:
● 2—2½×42" strips

From cream print, cut:
● 2—2½×42" strips

From purple print, cut:
● 4—1½×22½" sashing strips
● 8—1½×6½" sashing strips

From black plaid, cut:
● 4—2½×42" binding strips
● 4—1½×30½" sashing strips
● 4—1½×4½" sashing strips

From solid off-white, cut:
● 1 of Pattern A
● 2 of Pattern B

From dark brown print, cut:
● 1 of Pattern C

From black check, cut:
● 1 *each* of patterns D and E

From gold print, cut:
● 1 of Pattern F
● 2 of Pattern G

From lavender print, cut:
● 1 of Pattern H

From tomato red print, cut:
● 1 of Pattern I

From solid black, cut:
● 1 of Pattern J

From rust and gold prints, cut:
● 4 of Pattern K

From solid green, cut:
● 4 of Pattern L

From green print, cut:
● 4 of Pattern L

appliqué the center foundation

1. When the appliqué pieces are prepared, arrange them on the antique gold print 24×16" foundation rectangle (see the Quilt Assembly Diagram on *page 15*); baste in place.

2. Using threads in colors that match the fabrics, appliqué the pieces in place.

3. Using one thread of dark brown embroidery floss, stem-stitch the nose, mouth, upper eye line, and eyebrow. (For specific instructions on stem stitching, see Embroidery Stitches on *page 93*.)

4. Using one strand of dark brown embroidery floss, add a French knot for each eye. (For specific instructions on French knots, see Embroidery Stitches.)

5. Dip a small, round stencil brush into acrylic paint; rub the excess into a paper towel. When the paint begins to have a powder-like appearance, apply it to the cheek area of the face. If the quilt will be washed, throw it into the dryer at this point to heat-set the paint.

6. Trim the appliquéd foundation to measure 22½×14½", including the seam allowances.

embellish the appliquéd foundation

1. Lay a solid green L triangle atop a green print L triangle.

2. Stitch around the triangle, leaving a ¾" opening on one side for turning. Trim the seam allowance to ⅛", turn right side out, and press to make a pinwheel unit. Stitch the opening closed.

3. Repeat steps 1 and 2 to make a total of four pinwheel units.

4. Place the four pinwheel units at the top of the appliquéd pinwheel stick so they form a square. Fold the left outer corner of each pinwheel unit toward the center and tack it in place.

5. Hand-stitch the pinwheel in place, then stitch a button to the center of the pinwheel.

6. Thread your needle with gold thread; tie a heavy knot at the end. Take running stitches (approximately four per inch) all the way around a rust or gold print circle, ⅛" away from the edge; do not turn the edge under (see Diagram 3, *above right*). If your stitches are too small or too far away from the edge, you won't be able to gather the fabric smoothly.

7. Pull the thread, gathering the edge to the center with the wrong side of the fabric hidden inside, to make a yo-yo (see Diagram 4).

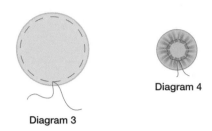

Diagram 3   **Diagram 4**

8. Repeat steps 6 and 7 to make a total of four yo-yos. Tack the yo-yos in place on the appliquéd foundation.

assemble the star units

1. Sew together one tomato red print triangle and one dark cream print triangle to make a triangle-square (see Diagram 5). Press the seam allowance toward the red triangle. The pieced triangle-square should measure 2½" square, including the seam allowances. Repeat to make a total of 24 triangle-squares.

Diagram 5

2. Referring to Diagram 6, lay out four triangle-squares, a tomato red print 2½" square, and four terra-cotta print 2½" squares in rows. Join the squares in each row. Press the seam allowances toward the red and terra-cotta squares. Then join the rows to make a star block. The star block should measure 6½" square, including the seam allowances. Repeat to make a total of six star blocks.

Diagram 6

3. Referring to Diagram 7, *opposite*, lay out three star blocks and four purple print 1½×6½" sashing strips in a row. Sew

together. Press the seam allowances toward the purple sashing strips. Then add a purple print 1½×22½" sashing strip to each long edge of the star row to make a star unit. The pieced star unit should measure 8½×22½", including the seam allowances. Repeat to make a second star unit.

assemble the checkerboard units

1. Sew together one taupe print 2½×42" strip and one cream print 2½×42" strip to make a strip set (see Diagram 8). Press the seam allowance toward the taupe print strip. Repeat to make a second strip set.

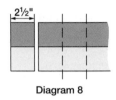

Diagram 8

2. Cut the strip sets into a total of 28 2½"-wide segments.

3. Join fourteen 2½"-wide segments in a row, alternating the color placement, to make a checkerboard strip. The pieced checkerboard strip should measure 4½×28½", including the seam allowances. Repeat to make a second checkerboard strip.

4. Sew a black plaid 1½×4½" sashing strip to each short end of the checkerboard strips. Then add a black plaid 1½×30½" sashing strip to each long edge of the checkerboard strips to make two checkerboard border units. Press all seam allowances toward the black strips. Each pieced checkerboard border unit should measure 6½×30½", including the seam allowances.

assemble the quilt top

1. Sew the star units to the top and bottom edges of the appliquéd foundation. Press the seam allowances toward the appliquéd foundation.

2. Sew the checkerboard units to the side edges of the appliquéd foundation to complete the quilt top.

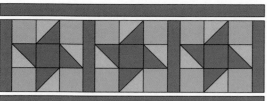

Diagram 7

complete the quilt

1. Layer the quilt top, batting, and backing according to the instructions in Quilting Basics, which begins on *page 94*.

2. Quilt as desired. Miriam outlined the angel, pinwheel, and appliqué foundation with terra-cotta floss. She used tan floss to stitch diagonally through the checkerboard squares with large Xs, and she outline-stitched around the red stars with tan floss.

3. Use the black plaid 2½×42" strips to bind the quilt according to the instructions in Quilting Basics.

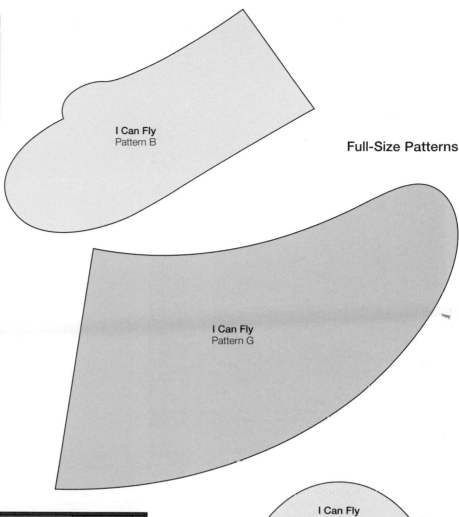

I Can Fly
Pattern B

Full-Size Patterns

I Can Fly
Pattern G

I Can Fly
Pattern A

Quilt Assembly Diagram

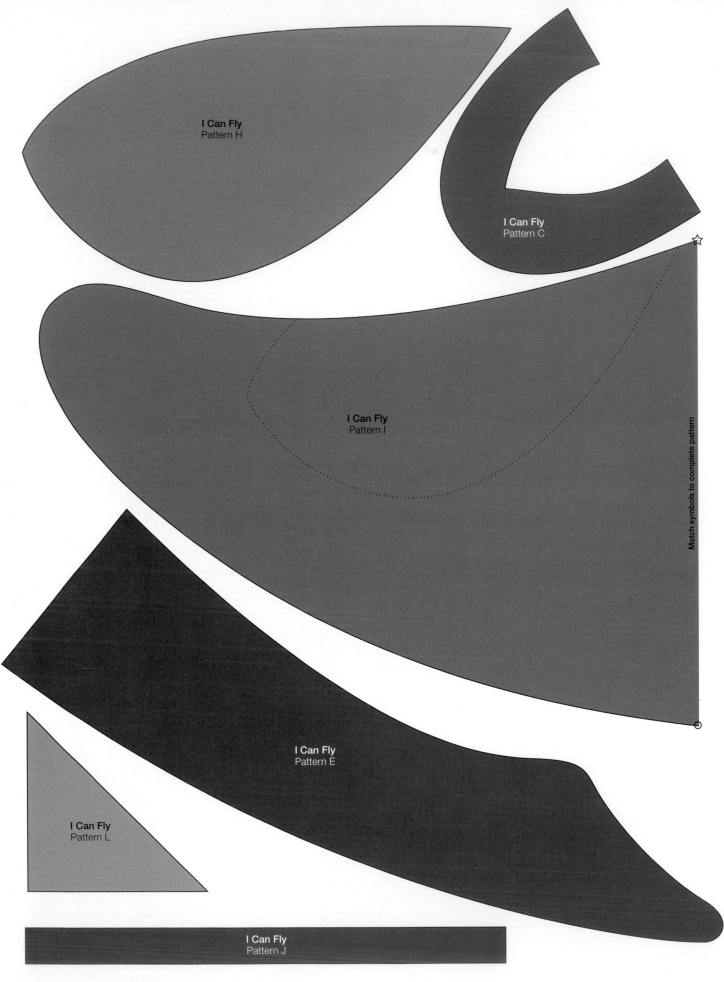

I Can Fly
Pattern H

I Can Fly
Pattern C

I Can Fly
Pattern I

Match symbols to complete pattern

I Can Fly
Pattern E

I Can Fly
Pattern L

I Can Fly
Pattern J

Full-Size Patterns

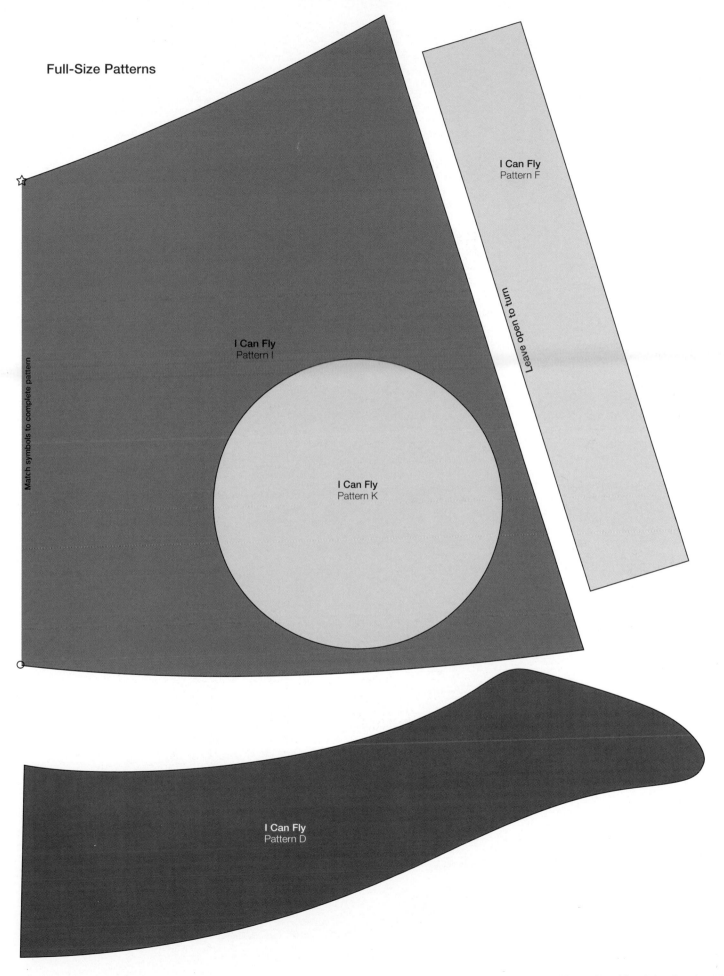

Match symbols to complete pattern

I Can Fly
Pattern F

Leave open to turn

I Can Fly
Pattern I

I Can Fly
Pattern K

I Can Fly
Pattern D

looking back

Red-and-gold flowers sprout from large Ohio Stars in this scrappy adaptation of an antique crib quilt.

Designer: Alice Berg
Photographer: Perry Struse

materials

⅝ yard of red print No. 1 for blocks

¾ yard of gold print No. 1 for blocks and appliqué stems

⅞ yard total of assorted red prints for blocks

⅞ yard total of assorted gold prints for blocks

¼ yard of red print No. 2 for flower appliqués

¼ yard of dark red print for sashing

1½ yards of red print No. 3 for sawtooth border and binding

⅞ yard of green check for border

3¼ yards of backing fabric

58" square of quilt batting

FINISHED QUILT TOP: 52" square
FINISHED BLOCK: 20" square

Quantities specified for 44/45"-wide, 100% cotton fabrics. All measurements include a ¼" seam allowance. Sew with right sides together unless otherwise stated.

cut the fabrics

To make the best use of your fabrics, cut the pieces in the order that follows. The red print No. 3 border strips are cut the length of the fabric (parallel to the selvage).

The patterns are on *page 21*. To make templates of the patterns, follow the instructions in Appliqué Primer, which begins on *page 84*.

From red print No. 1, cut:
● 8—8⅜" squares, cutting each in half diagonally for a total of 16 triangles

From gold print No. 1, cut:
● 8—8⅜" squares, cutting each in half diagonally for a total of 16 triangles
● 16—1½×6" strips

From assorted red prints, cut:
● 4—5½" squares
● 1—1½" square
● 8—1" squares

From assorted gold prints, cut:
● 4—5½" squares
● 4—1" squares
● 4—1×1½" rectangles

From assorted red prints and gold prints, cut:
● 48—3×5½" rectangles
● 96—3" squares

From red print No. 2, cut:
● 32 *each* of patterns A and A reversed
● 16 of Pattern B

From dark red print, cut:
● 4—2½×20½" sashing strips

From red print No. 3, cut:
● 5—2½×52" binding strips
● 4—1½×52½" border strips

From green check, cut:
● 4—5½×42½" border strips

assemble the blocks

1. Finger-press each red print triangle in half to create an appliqué placement guide.

2. With the wrong side inside, fold each gold print 1½×6" strip in thirds; press.

3. Using gold thread, appliqué a pressed gold print strip to each red print triangle along the placement guide (see Diagram 1).

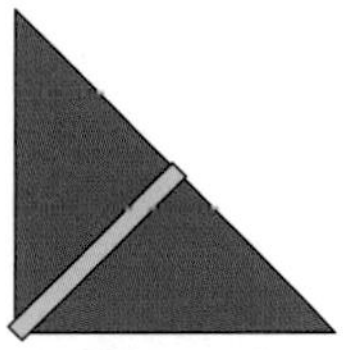

Diagram 1

4. Sew together one appliquéd red print triangle and one gold print triangle to make a triangle-square (see Diagram 2). Press the seam allowance toward the red print triangle. The pieced triangle-square should measure 8" square, including the seam allowances. Repeat to make a total of 16 triangle-squares.

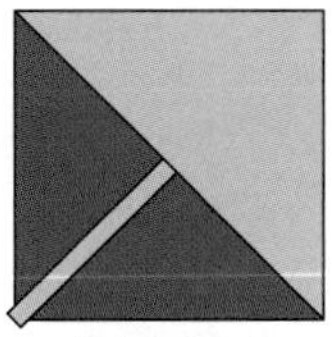

Diagram 2

5. For accurate sewing lines, use a quilting pencil to mark a diagonal line on the back of each assorted red print and gold print 3" square. (To prevent your fabric from stretching as you draw the lines, place 220-grit sandpaper under the squares.)

6. Align a marked red or gold print 3" square with one end of a gold or red print 3×5½" rectangle (see Diagram 3). Sew on the drawn line; trim and press. Add a second marked red or gold print 3" square to the opposite end of the rectangle in the same manner to make a Flying Geese unit. The pieced Flying Geese unit should still measure 3×5½", including the seam allowances. Repeat with the remaining marked red and gold 3" squares and 3×5½" rectangles to make a total of 48 Flying Geese units.

Diagram 3

7. Referring to Diagram 4 for placement, sew together three Flying Geese units to make a Flying Geese block. Press the seam allowances in one direction. The pieced Flying Geese block should measure 5½×8", including the seam allowances. Repeat to make a total of 16 Flying Geese blocks.

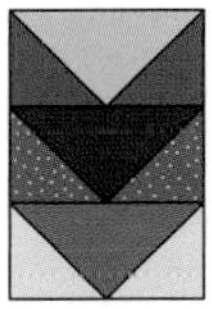

Diagram 4

8. Referring to Diagram 5 on *page 20* for placement, lay out four triangle-squares, four Flying Geese blocks, and one red print 5½" square in three horizontal rows. Sew together the pieces in each row. Press the seam allowances toward the triangle-squares in the top and bottom rows and toward the red print square in the middle row. Then join the rows to make a pieced block. Press the seam allowances in one direction. The pieced block should measure 20½" square, including the seam allowances. Repeat to make a total of four blocks.

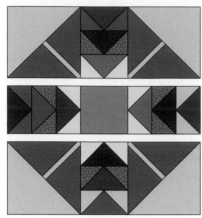

Diagram 5

9. Referring to the photograph *opposite* for placement, lay out two red print A leaves, two red print A reversed leaves, and one red print B circle in each corner of the pieced blocks. Using red thread, appliqué the pieces in place to complete each block. Always work from the bottom layer to the top when appliquéing.

assemble the quilt center

1. Use a quilting pencil to mark a diagonal line on the back of each assorted red print 1" square.

2. Align a marked red print 1" square with one end of a gold print 1×1½" rectangle (see Diagram 3 on *page 19*). Sew on the drawn line; trim and press. Add a second marked red print 1" square to the opposite end of the gold print rectangle in the same manner to make a Flying Geese unit. The pieced Flying Geese unit should still measure 1×1½", including the seam allowances. Repeat to make a total of four Flying Geese units.

3. Referring to Diagram 6, *above right*, for placement, lay out the four Flying Geese units, the four gold print 1" squares, and the red print 1½" square in three horizontal rows. Sew together the pieces in each row. Press the seam allowances toward the gold or red print squares. Then join the rows to make an Ohio Star block. The pieced Ohio Star block should measure 2½" square, including the seam allowances.

Diagram 6

4. Referring to the photograph *opposite* for placement, lay out the four pieced and appliquéd blocks, the four dark red print 2½×20½" sashing strips, and the pieced Ohio Star block in three horizontal rows. Sew together the pieces in each row. Press the seam allowances toward the sashing strips. Then join the rows to complete the quilt center. Press the seam allowances toward the sashing strips. The pieced quilt center should measure 42½" square, including the seam allowances.

add the border

1. Sew the green check 5½×42½" border strips to opposite edges of the pieced quilt center. Press the seam allowances toward the green check border.

2. Add a gold print 5½" square to each end of the remaining green check 5½×42½" border strips to make two border units. Press the seam allowances toward the green check strips.

3. Join the border units to the remaining edges of the pieced quilt center. Press the seam allowances toward the green check border.

4. Referring to Diagram 7, use a quilting pencil to mark the red print 1½×52½" border strips at 2" intervals. Mark a ¼" seam allowance along one long edge of each strip.

Diagram 7

5. Cut the strips on the marked 2" intervals, stopping at the marked seam allowance (see Diagram 8).

Diagram 8

6. Referring to Diagram 9, diagonally fold under one side of a 2"-wide flap; fold under the other side of the flap to make a sawtooth point; press. Baste the point in place. Repeat with each 2"-wide flap along each strip.

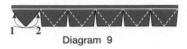

Diagram 9

7. With right sides facing up, place a basted sawtooth border strip atop a green check border; align raw edges. Appliqué the sawtooth points in place. Repeat with the remaining sawtooth border strips to complete the quilt top.

complete the quilt

1. Layer the quilt top, batting, and backing according to the instructions in Quilting Basics, which begins on *page 94*.

2. Quilt as desired. Designer Alice Berg hand-quilted a 1"-wide grid in the border. She also outline-quilted inside each Flying Geese unit and inside the appliqué pieces.

3. Use the red print 2½×52" strips to bind the quilt according to the instructions in Quilting Basics.

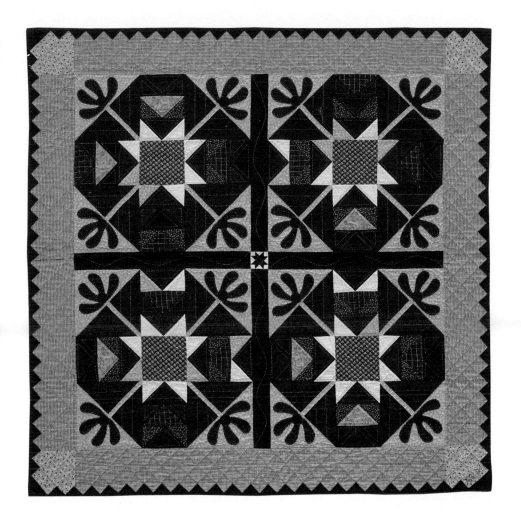

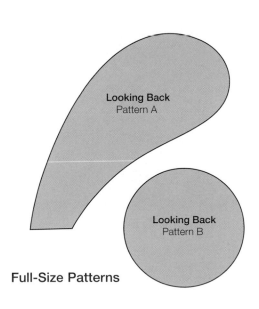

Full-Size Patterns

Looking Back
Pattern A

Looking Back
Pattern B

COLOR OPTION
Hues in purple and tan give this smaller rendition a lighter feel. Using just one block for the quilt, the center star motif is pieced with a print of purple flowers on a tan background and combines with several purple prints, one green print, and a light cream print to complete the palette.

morning
glories

Four string-pieced triangles form the foundation for a primitive wreath of appliquéd morning glories. A quilt-as-you-appliqué method makes assembly easy.

Designer: Kris Kerrigan   Photographer: Perry Struse

materials

½ yard of solid green for vine and leaf
  appliqués
⅛ yard of blue plaid for flower appliqués
⅛ yard of pale yellow print for star
  appliqués
12—⅛-yard pieces of assorted beige
  prints for appliqué foundation
¼ yard of brown check for border
⅝ yard of navy stripe for bow and
  binding
28" square of backing fabric
28" square of quilt batting
Embroidery floss: green
Quilting thread: black
Paper or tear-away stabilizer
Freezer paper (optional)

FINISHED QUILT TOP: 21½" square

Quantities specified for 44/45"-wide,
100% cotton fabrics. All measurements
include a ¼" seam allowance. Sew with
right sides together unless otherwise
stated.

cut the fabrics

To make the best use of your fabrics, cut the
pieces in the order that follows. The patterns
are on *page 24*. To use freezer-paper templates
for appliquéing, as was done in this project,
complete the following steps.

1. Position the freezer paper, shiny side
down, over the patterns. With a pencil, trace
each pattern the number of times indicated.
Cut out the freezer-paper templates on the
traced lines.

2. Place a small amount of fabric glue on the
matte side of the freezer-paper templates
and anchor them onto the backs of the
designated fabrics, leaving approximately ½"
between templates for seam allowances. Cut
out the fabric appliqué pieces about ¼"
beyond the freezer-paper edges.

3. Use the point of a hot, dry iron to fold
under and press the seam allowances onto
the shiny side of the freezer-paper template.
Clip curves as necessary.

From solid green, cut:
● 2—¾×22" bias strips (For specific
  instructions on cutting bias strips,
  see Appliqué Primer, which begins on
  page 84.)
● 14 of Pattern A
From blue plaid, cut:
● 8 of Pattern B
From pale yellow print, cut:
● 8 of Pattern C
From assorted beige prints, cut:
● 18—42" long strips, varying in width
  from 1" to 1¾"-wide
From brown check, cut:
● 4—1½×25" border strips
From navy stripe, cut:
● 3—2½×42" binding strips
● 1—1½×15½" bias strip
From paper stabilizer, cut:
● 2—14⅞" squares, cutting each in half
  diagonally for a total of 4 triangles

assemble the quilt top

1. Lay a beige print strip right side up
diagonally across the corner of a paper or
tear-away stabilizer triangle. Make sure that
the strip completely covers the triangle's
corner.

2. With raw edges aligned, lay a second
beige print 1½×42" strip atop the first. Sew
together, sewing through the paper (see
Diagram 1). Press the attached strip open.

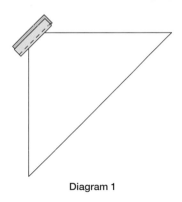

Diagram 1

3. Lay a third beige print 1½×42" strip atop
the second strip. Join and press as before.
Continue adding strips in the same manner
until the paper triangle is completely covered.

4. Trim the pieced strips so each short edge
of the string-pieced triangle measures 14⅞"
long (see Diagram 2).

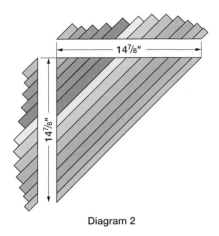

Diagram 2

5. Repeat steps 1 through 4 to make a total
of four string-pieced triangles.

6. Aligning the midpoints, add a brown
check 1½×25" border strip to each string-
pieced triangle's long edge. Trim the ends
even with the string-pieced triangle.

7. Sew together the string-pieced triangles
in pairs (see Diagram 3). Press the seam
allowances in opposite directions. Then join
the pairs to make the quilt top. Carefully
remove the paper.

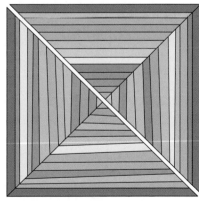

Diagram 3

complete the quilt

1. Layer the quilt top, batting, and backing according to the instructions in Quilting Basics, which begins on *page 94*. Quilt as desired.

2. Use the navy stripe 2½×42" strips to bind the quilt according to the instructions in Quilting Basics.

3. Press under ¼" of each long edge of the two solid green ¾×22" bias strips to prepare the vines.

4. Referring to the photograph on *page 22* for placement, pin the two prepared vines to the quilt top. The vines should begin and end approximately 3¼" from the quilt top's edges. Baste the vines in place.

5. Arrange the prepared flower, star, and leaf appliqués along the vine. When you're pleased with the arrangement, baste all pieces in place.

6. Knot the end of an 18" length of black quilting thread and straight-stitch a blue plaid flower appliqué to the quilt top, stitching through all layers.

To straight stitch, start with your needle underneath the flower appliqué and ¼" inside the flower's edge; bring your needle to the top, hiding the knot below the appliqué piece (see Straight Stitch diagram *below*). Bring the needle down at the edge of the appliqué, keeping your stitches perpendicular to the folded edge and ⅛" to ¼" apart. They'll resemble blanket stitches, although the thread won't run parallel to the appliqué. Repeat with all the appliqué pieces.

Straight Stitch

7. Using black quilting thread, backstitch a curved line below each appliquéd star, stitching through all layers.

To backstitch, pull your needle up at A (see Backstitch diagram *below*). Insert it back into the fabric at B, and bring it up at C. Push your needle down again at D, and bring it up at E. Continue in the same manner.

Backstitch

8. Using three strands of green embroidery floss, stem-stitch a stem for each appliquéd leaf, stitching through all layers.

To stem-stitch, pull your needle up at A (see Stem Stitch diagram *below*). Insert the needle into the fabric at B, about ⅜" away from A. Holding the floss out of the way, bring the needle up at C and pull the floss through so it lies flat against the fabric. The distances between points A, B, and C should be equal. Pull with equal tautness after each stitch.

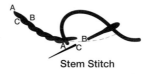

Stem Stitch

9. Fold the navy stripe 1½×15½" bias strip in half lengthwise with the right side inside. Sew the long edges together to make a tube. Turn the tube right side out. Press with the seam on a folded edge. Turn the raw ends to the inside of the tube at an angle. Sew along the angled ends. Tie the tube into a bow. Tack the bow where the vines overlap at the bottom to complete the quilt.

Morning Glories
Pattern A

Morning Glories
Pattern B

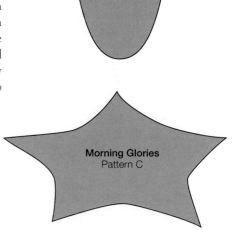

Morning Glories
Pattern C

Full-Size Patterns

Celebrate
the beauty
of the
outdoors
with climbing
vines and
leaves
appliquéd in
1930s
reproduction
fabrics.

Designers:
Becky Goldsmith and
Linda Jenkins

Photographer:
Hopkins Associates

gathering
leaves

materials

3 yards of solid light green for
   appliqué foundations
1½ yards of tan-and-green plaid
   for sashing
1½ yards of red print for inner border
1½ yards of green print for outer border
½ yard *total* of assorted green, red,
   yellow, blue, brown, purple, and
   pink prints for leaf appliqués
1⅝ yards of dark green print for
   vine appliqués and cording cover
3 yards of backing fabric
53×63" of quilt batting
2 yards of clear upholstery vinyl
   or other clear flexible
   plastic (optional)
6¼ yards of ¼"-wide cotton or
   polyester cording
⅜" bias bar

FINISHED QUILT TOP: 47×57"

Quantities specified for 44/45"-wide,
100% cotton fabrics. All measurements
include a ¼" seam allowance. Sew with
right sides together unless otherwise
stated.

cut the fabrics

To make the best use of your fabrics, cut the
pieces in the order that follows. The Leaf
Pattern is on *page 27*. To make a template of
the pattern, follow the instructions in
Appliqué Primer, which begins on *page 84*.
Cut the border and sashing strips lengthwise
(parallel to the selvage).

From solid light green, cut:
- 3—14×50" rectangles for appliqué
   foundations

From tan-and-green plaid, cut:
- 4—1½×48½" sashing strips
- 2—1½×40½" sashing strips

From red print, cut:
- 2—1×50½" inner border strips
- 2—1×41½" inner border strips

From medium green print, cut:
- 2—3½×51½" outer border strips
- 2—3½×47½" outer border strips

**From assorted green, red, yellow, blue,
brown, purple, and pink prints, cut:**
- 48 of Leaf Pattern

From dark green print, cut:
- 1—26" square, cutting it into enough
   2½"-wide bias strips to total 220" for
   cording cover
- 1—25" square, cutting it into enough
   1½"-wide bias strips to make three
   65"-long strips for vines (For specific
   instructions, see Cutting Bias Strips in
   Appliqué Primer.)

make the bias vines

1. Sew the dark green print 1½"-wide bias
strips end to end into three 65"-long strips.

2. With wrong sides together, lightly press
each dark green print 1½×65" bias strip in
half lengthwise.

3. With the folded edge on the machine
seam guide and using a scant ⅜" seam
allowance, stitch the length of each strip to
make vines. Trim away the seam allowances,
leaving only enough fabric to hold each vine
intact.

4. Slide the ⅜" bias bar into a vine, wiggle
the seam to a flat side of the bar, and press
the seam allowance to one side so that both
the seam allowance and the seam are hidden.
Remove the bar from the vine and press the
vine again. Repeat with the remaining vines.

make the full-size patterns

1. Draw a 12×48" rectangle on white paper.
Repeat to make a total of three 12×48"
rectangles.

2. With a pencil, mark a line 3" in from each
long side of a rectangle. These lines
represent the vine boundaries. The leaves
can extend beyond these boundaries but
must be kept at least ½" from the raw edges.

3. Tape the lined paper rectangle near the
edge of a countertop or table.

4. Draw the curves of a vine with the pencil
from one short end of the rectangle to the
other. Remember to stay in the center of
the rectangle. Draw a second line ⅜" away
from the first line to show the actual
thickness of the vine.

5. Repeat steps two through four on the
remaining two paper rectangles, starting
each vine in a slightly different location. It is
important that the vine panels are different
from one another. The subtle differences in
the curves of each vine make your quilt
much more interesting to view.

6. Using the leaf template and a pencil,
trace leaves along each drawn vine to
complete the vine-and-leaf patterns.

appliqué the center

1. Prepare leaves for appliqué by finger-
pressing the 3/16" seam allowances under.

2. Cut a 12×48" rectangle of clear
upholstery vinyl. Position the vinyl or plastic
rectangle over a drawn vine-and-leaf pattern
and accurately trace the design with a
permanent marker.

3. Position the overlay on a solid light green
foundation rectangle. Pin the top of the
overlay to the fabric, if desired.

4. Slide a dark green print vine, right side
up, between the foundation rectangle and
the overlay. Vines can be tricky to position;
take your time and work in sections. Be sure
excess vine trails off the foundation
rectangle at each short edge.

5. When the vine is in place, remove the
overlay, pin the vine to the foundation, and
appliqué it in place.

6. Place the overlay on the foundation
rectangle again. Working down the vine,
position 16 leaves under the overlay, remove
the overlay, pin or baste the leaves to the
foundation, and appliqué them in place.

7. Trim the appliquéd foundation rectangle
to 12½×48½", including the seam allowances.

8. Repeat steps 2 through 7 with the
remaining light green foundation rectangles
and drawn vine-and-leaf patterns.

assemble the quilt center

1. Referring to the photograph on *page 25* for placement, lay out the three appliquéd rectangles and four tan-and-green plaid 1½×48½" sashing strips, alternating the appliquéd rectangles and sashing strips. Join the pieces; press the seam allowances toward the tan-and-green plaid sashing strips.

2. Sew the tan-and-green plaid 1½×40½" sashing strip to the top and bottom edges to complete the quilt center. Press the seam allowances toward the sashing strips. The pieced quilt center should measure 40½×50½", including the seam allowances.

add the borders

1. Sew the red print 1×50½" inner border strips to the side edges of the pieced quilt center. Then sew the red print 1×41½" inner border strips to the top and bottom edges of the pieced quilt center. Press the seam allowances toward the red print border.

2. Sew the medium green print 3½×51½" outer border strips to the side edges of the pieced quilt center. Then sew the medium green print 3½×47½" outer border strips to the top and bottom edges of the pieced quilt center to complete the quilt top. Press the seam allowances toward the medium green print border.

complete the quilt

1. Sew the dark green print 2½"-wide bias strips end to end into one 220"-long strip.

2. With wrong sides together, fold under 1½" at one end of the strip. With wrong sides together, fold the strip in half lengthwise to make the cording cover. Insert the cording next to the folded edge, placing it 1" from the folded end. Using a machine cording foot, sew through both strip layers right next to the cording.

3. Starting on the lower right side of the quilt top, align raw edges and stitch the covered cording to the right side of the quilt top. Begin stitching 1½" from the cording's folded end. Round the corners slightly, making sure the curve of each corner matches the others. As you stitch each corner, gently push the covered cording into place.

4. After going around the edge of the quilt top, cut the end of the cording so that it will fit snugly into the folded opening at the beginning. The ends of the cording should abut inside the dark green print cover. Stitch the ends down and trim raw edges as needed.

5. Layer the quilt top, batting, and backing according to the instructions in Quilting Basics, which begins on *page 94*.

6. Quilt everything but the outside border as desired. This quilt was hand-quilted in an echo pattern as shown in the detail photograph *below*.

7. Trim the batting even with the cording seam line. Trim the backing even with the outer raw edge of the quilt top, ¼" larger than the batting on all sides. Fold the cording cover's seam allowance over the batting. Fold under the quilt backing; whipstitch the edges together. Quilt the outside border.

Gathering Leaves
Leaf Pattern

Full-Size Pattern

noah's
garden

Cultivate the cheery rows of rotary-cut and
appliquéd vegetables on this fun and bright quilt.

Designer: Stephanie Martin   Photographer: Perry Struse

materials

FOR CORN ROW:
⅛ yard *each* of prints in yellow, tan, light green, dark green, and green
⅛ yard solid blue
FOR PEPPER ROW:
8—4" squares of solids shading from light yellow to orange
Scrap of solid light green
32½×4½" strip of solid dark green
FOR CARROT ROW:
⅜ yard of brown print
⅛ yard of light green print
⅛ yard of orange print
FOR TOMATO ROW:
8—4" squares of solids shading from light red to dark red
32½×4½" strip of solid lime green
FOR RADISH ROW:
⅜ yard of burgundy print
¼ yard of green print
¼ yard of red stripe
FOR FINISHING:
1⅜ yards of light green print for border
1½ yards of green geometric print for border
⅛ yard of red print for appliqués
⅜ yard of solid green for binding
2 yards of backing fabric
46×50" of quilt batting
Embroidery floss: green

FINISHED QUILT TOP: 39×43½"

Quantities specified for 44/45"-wide, 100% cotton fabrics. All measurements include a ¼" seam allowance. Sew with right sides together unless otherwise stated.

cut and assemble the vegetable rows

To make the best use of your fabrics, cut the pieces in the order listed in each of the following sections. The patterns begin on *page 31*. To make templates of the patterns, follow the instructions in Appliqué Primer, which begins on *page 84*.

CORN
From yellow print, cut:
● 8 of Pattern A
From tan print, cut:
● 8 of Pattern D

From light green print, cut:
● 8 of Pattern E
From dark green print, cut:
● 8 of Pattern E reversed
From green print, cut:
● 8 of Pattern C
From solid blue, cut:
● 8 *each* of patterns B, B reversed, F, and F reversed

1. Referring to Diagram 1 for placement, lay out the pieces. Sew together the pieces in sections as shown. Then join the sections to make a corn unit (see Diagram 2). Press the seam allowances in one direction. The pieced corn unit should measure 4½×9½", including the seam allowances. Repeat to make a total of eight corn units.

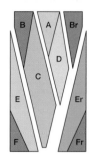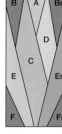

Diagram 1   Diagram 2

2. Sew together the eight corn units in a horizontal row to make a corn row. Press the seam allowances in one direction. The pieced corn row should measure 32½×9½", including the seam allowances.

PEPPERS
From *each* 4" square shading from light yellow to orange, cut:
● 1 of Pattern G
From solid light green, cut:
● 8 of Pattern H

1. Lay out the G and H pepper shapes on the solid dark green 32½×4½" strip; baste or pin in place so that a pepper will be directly below each corn unit.

2. Using threads that match the fabrics, appliqué the pepper pieces to the dark green strip to make a pepper row.

CARROTS
From brown print, cut:
● 1 *each* of patterns M and M reversed
● 7 *each* of patterns O and L
● 1 *each* of patterns I and I reversed
● 8 of Pattern K
From light green print, cut:
● 8 *each* of patterns J and J reversed
From orange print, cut:
● 8 of Pattern N

1. Referring to Diagram 3 for placement, lay out the pieces for the carrot top row. Sew together the pieces in sections as shown. Press the seam allowances. Then join the sections to make a row. The pieced carrot top row should measure 32½×4¼", including the seam allowances.

Diagram 3

2. Lay out the pieces for the carrot bottom row (see Diagram 4). Sew together the pieces to make a horizontal row. Press the seam allowances. The pieced carrot bottom row should measure 32½×6¼", including the seam allowances.

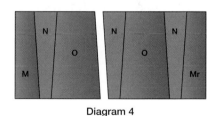

Diagram 4

3. Join the carrot top and carrot bottom rows. Press the seam allowance toward the carrot bottom row. The pieced carrot row should measure 32½×10", including the seam allowances.

TOMATOES
From *each* 4" square shading from solid light red to solid dark red, cut:
● 1 of Pattern P

1. Lay out the tomato shapes on the solid lime green 32½×4½" strip; baste or pin in place. With thread that matches the fabric, appliqué the shapes to the lime green strip to make the tomato row.

2. Using the lazy daisy stitch and two strands of green embroidery floss, add tomato stems. (For specific instructions on the lazy daisy stitch, refer to Embroidery Stitches on *page 93.*) Embroider three lazy daisy stitches on each tomato.

RADISHES
From burgundy print, cut:
- 1—32½×4½" strip
- 1 *each* of patterns Q and Q reversed
- 7 of Pattern S

From green print, cut:
- 8 of Pattern R

From red stripe, cut:
- 8 of Pattern T

1. Referring to Diagram 5 for placement, lay out the pieces for the radish top row. Sew together the pieces in sections as shown. Press the seam allowances. The pieced radish top row should measure 32½×6½", including the seam allowances.

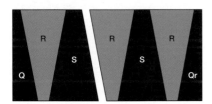

Diagram 5

2. Lay out the red stripe radish shapes on the burgundy print 32½×4½" strip; baste or pin in place. With thread that matches the fabric, appliqué the radish pieces to the burgundy strip to make the radish bottom row.

3. Join the radish top and bottom rows to make the radish row. Press the seam allowance toward the top radish row. The pieced radish row should measure 32½×10½", including the seam allowances.

assemble the quilt center
1. Referring to the photograph *above right,* lay out the vegetable rows.

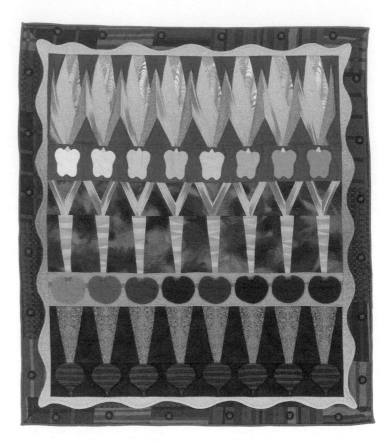

2. Sew together the rows to make the quilt center. Press the seam allowances in one direction. The pieced quilt center should measure 32½×37", including the seam allowances.

cut, assemble, and add the border
Cut the border strips lengthwise (parallel to the selvage).

From light green print, cut:
- 2—2×48" border strips
- 2—2×44½" border strips

From green geometric print, cut:
- 2—4×53" border strips
- 2—4×48" border strips

From red print, cut:
- 24 of Pattern U

1. Fold the lengthwise center of one light green strip. Align the center fold of the Appliqué Border Pattern, which begins on *page 34,* with the center of the light green strip. Moving the pattern along the strip, trace the scalloped edge; cut along the scalloped edge adding a ³⁄₁₆" seam allowance. Repeat with each remaining light green

strip. Turn under each strip's scalloped edge seam allowance; baste in place.

2. Match the straight raw edges of a scalloped border strip and a green geometric border strip of the same length; baste in place. Use matching thread to appliqué the curved edge in place, leaving 2" of the curved edge free at each end.

3. With midpoints aligned and referring to the photograph *above* for placement, sew the short green geometric border strips to the top and bottom edges of the quilt center and the long border strips to the side edges of the quilt center, mitering the corners with basting stitches. (For information on mitering, refer to Add the Outer Border instructions, beginning on *page 4.*) Before completing the miters, check to make sure the scalloped edges meet at each corner; adjust if necessary and baste in place. Remove the miter basting and appliqué the loose scalloped edges in place. Complete each mitered corner.

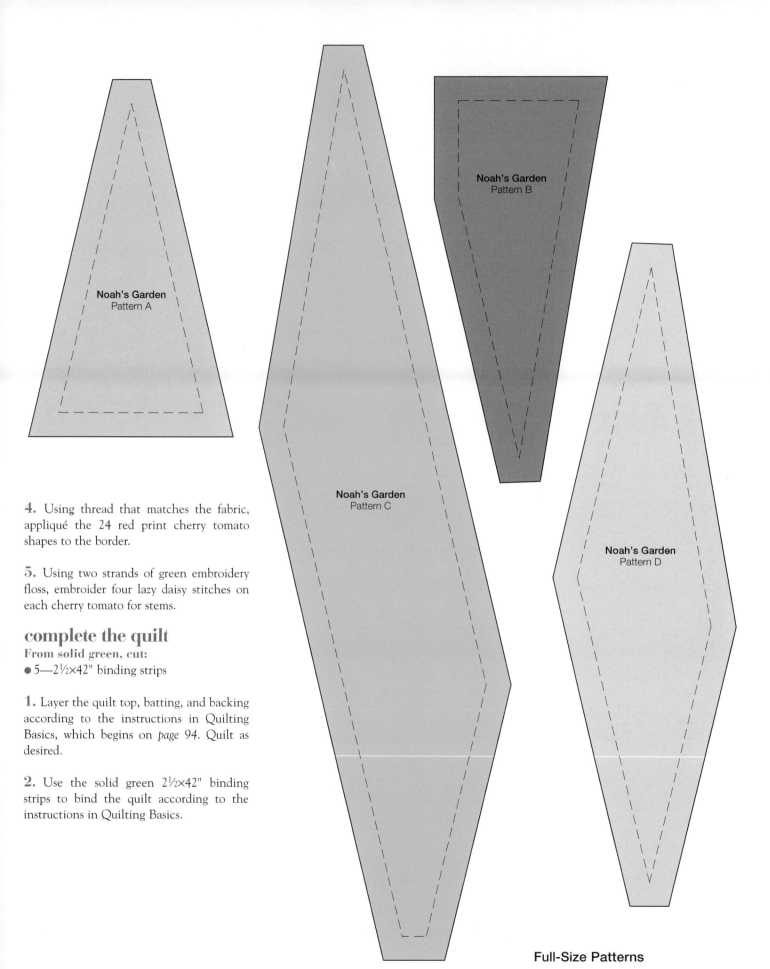

4. Using thread that matches the fabric, appliqué the 24 red print cherry tomato shapes to the border.

5. Using two strands of green embroidery floss, embroider four lazy daisy stitches on each cherry tomato for stems.

complete the quilt
From solid green, cut:
● 5—2½×42" binding strips

1. Layer the quilt top, batting, and backing according to the instructions in Quilting Basics, which begins on *page 94*. Quilt as desired.

2. Use the solid green 2½×42" binding strips to bind the quilt according to the instructions in Quilting Basics.

Noah's Garden
Pattern A

Noah's Garden
Pattern B

Noah's Garden
Pattern C

Noah's Garden
Pattern D

Full-Size Patterns

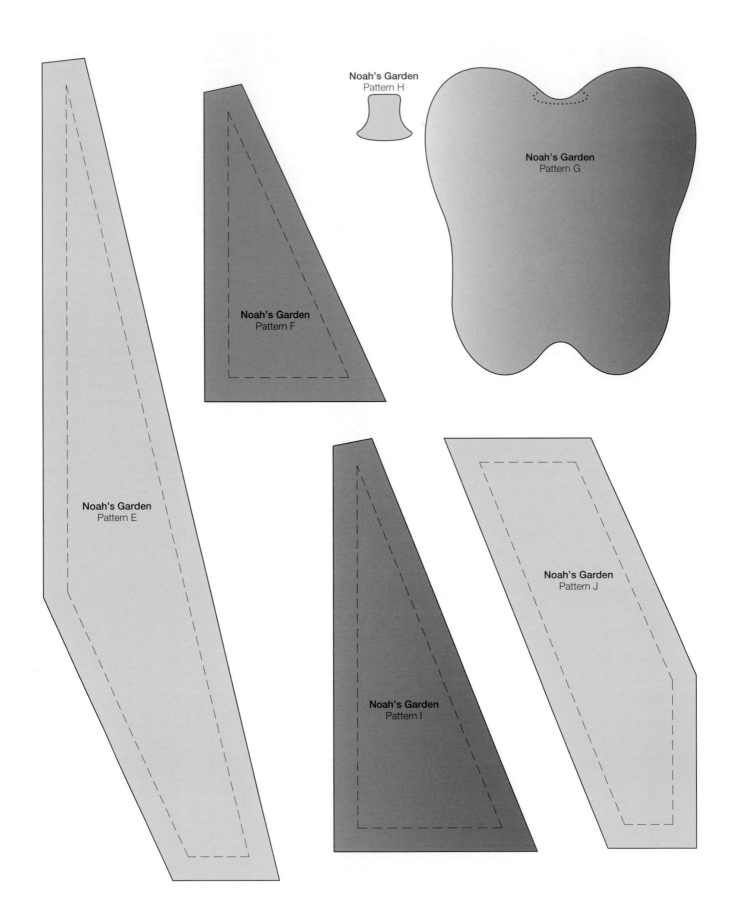

Noah's Garden
Pattern H

Noah's Garden
Pattern G

Noah's Garden
Pattern F

Noah's Garden
Pattern E

Noah's Garden
Pattern J

Noah's Garden
Pattern I

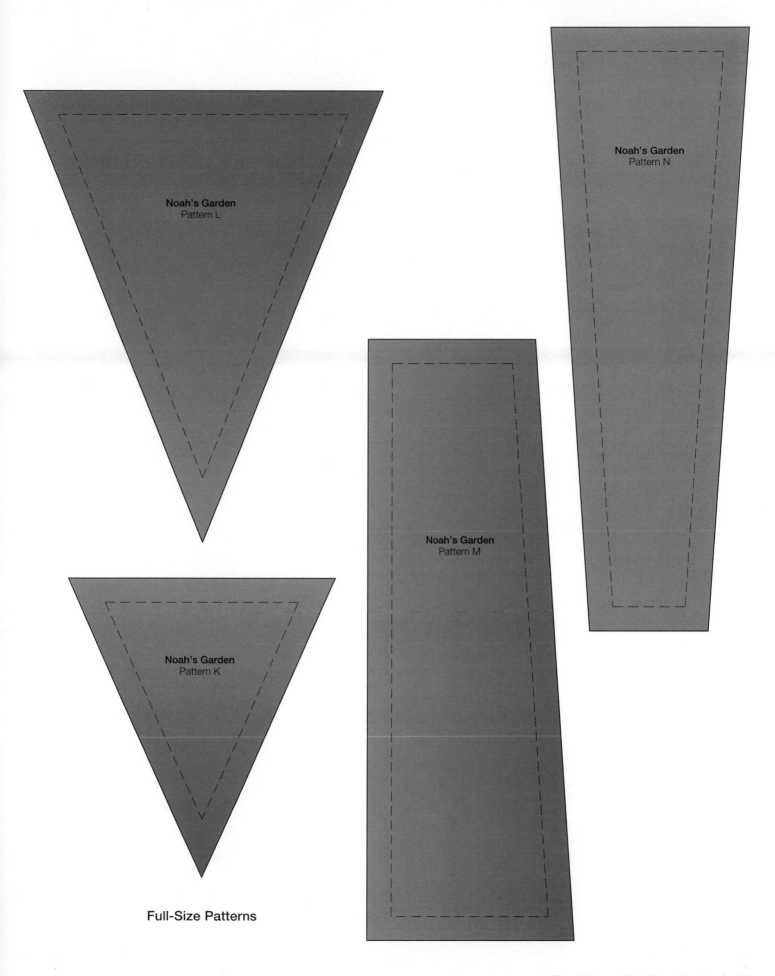

Noah's Garden
Pattern L

Noah's Garden
Pattern N

Noah's Garden
Pattern K

Noah's Garden
Pattern M

Full-Size Patterns

Full-Size Patterns

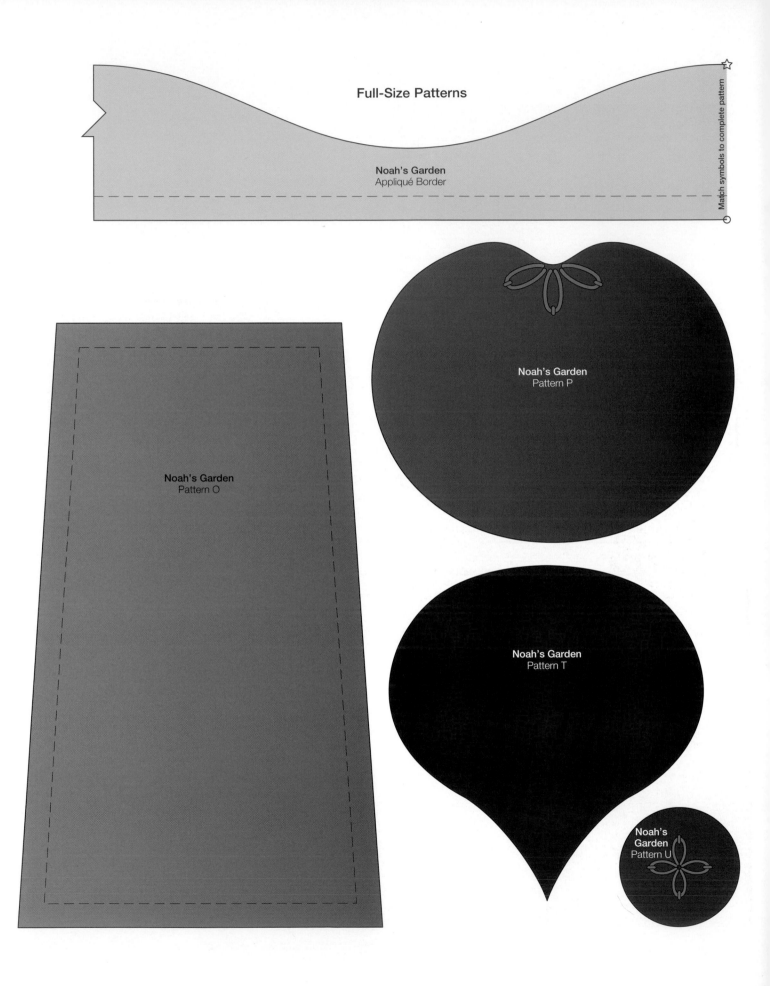

Match symbols to complete pattern

Noah's Garden
Appliqué Border

Noah's Garden
Pattern P

Noah's Garden
Pattern O

Noah's Garden
Pattern T

Noah's
Garden
Pattern U

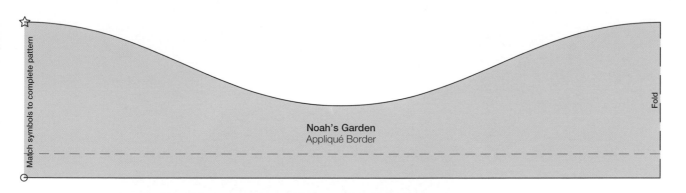

Match symbols to complete pattern

Noah's Garden
Appliqué Border

Fold

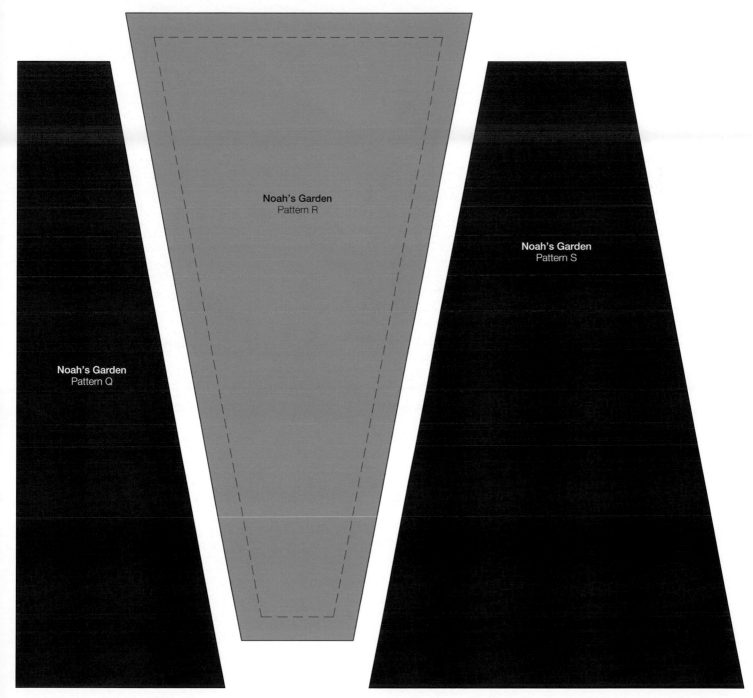

Noah's Garden
Pattern R

Noah's Garden
Pattern S

Noah's Garden
Pattern Q

perennial
patchwork

Appliqué simple, stylized flowers to create this wonderfully warm wall hanging. Its small size makes it a perfect take-along project.

Designer: Renée Plains   Photographer: Perry Struse

materials

- 1—12½×16½" rectangle of tan plaid for appliqué background
- 3—2½" squares of assorted red plaids for star appliqué foundations
- 2—1½×6½" rectangles of different brown prints for border
- Scraps of assorted black prints for appliqué vase and border
- Scraps of red plaid, dark rose plaid, mustard check, and red print for appliqués and pieced border
- 12" square of green check for appliqué vines and leaves
- 15" square of black plaid for binding
- 24×23" of backing fabric
- 24×23" of quilt batting
- Freezer paper

FINISHED QUILT TOP: 18×17"

Quantities specified for 44/45"-wide, 100% cotton fabrics. All measurements include a ¼" seam allowance. Sew with right sides together unless otherwise stated.

cut the fabrics

To make the best use of your fabrics, cut the pieces in the order that follows. The patterns are on *page 39*. To use freezer-paper templates for appliquéing, as was done in this project, complete the following steps.

1. Position the freezer paper, shiny side down, over the patterns. With a pencil, trace each pattern the number of times indicated. Cut out the freezer-paper templates on the traced lines.

2. Place a small amount of fabric glue on the matte side of the freezer-paper templates and anchor them onto the backs of the designated fabrics, leaving approximately ½" between templates for seam allowances. Cut out the fabric appliqué pieces about ¼" beyond the freezer-paper edges.

3. Use the point of a hot, dry iron to fold under and press the seam allowances onto the shiny side of the freezer-paper template. Clip curves as necessary.

From assorted black prints, cut:
- 2—1½ ×12½" border strips
- 2—1½×9½" strips
- 2—1½×6½" rectangles
- 1 of Pattern A

From red plaid, cut:
- 3 of Pattern N

From dark rose plaid, cut:
- 3 of Pattern O

From mustard check, cut:
- 4 of Pattern B
- 3 of Pattern P

From red print, cut:
- 1 *each* of patterns I, I reversed, M, and M reversed

From green check, cut:
- 1 *each* of patterns C, D, D reversed, E, E reversed, F, F reversed, G, G reversed, H, H reversed, J, J reversed, K, K reversed, L, and L reversed

From remaining assorted scraps, cut:
- 5—2½" squares
- 16—1½" squares

From black plaid, cut:
- Enough 2½"-wide bias strips to total 75" in length (For specific instructions, see Cutting Bias Strips in Appliqué Primer, which begins on *page 84*.)

appliqué the blocks

1. Press the ¼" seam allowance on all the appliqué pieces to the wrong side, using the freezer-paper templates as guides. Remove all freezer-paper templates. To obtain crisp folded edges, spray each appliqué piece with water or starch and press again.

2. Referring to the Appliqué Placement Diagram on *page 38*, lay out the appliqué pieces on the tan plaid 12½×16½" appliqué foundation, overlapping the pieces where necessary.

3. Using small slip stitches and threads that match the fabrics, appliqué the pieces to the foundation to make the center block. Gently press the block from the back.

4. In the same manner, appliqué each remaining mustard check B star atop an assorted red plaid 2½" square to make three star blocks.

assemble and add the borders

1. Sew the black print 1½×12½" border strip to each side edge of the appliquéd center block. Press the seam allowances toward the black print border.

2. Aligning short edges, sew together the two black print 1½×9½" strips to make the bottom border unit. Press the seam allowance open. Add the bottom border unit to the bottom edge of the appliquéd center block.

3. Aligning long edges, sew a black print 1½×6½" rectangle to a brown print 1½×6½" rectangle to make a pair. Repeat to make a second pair. Referring to Diagram 1 for placement, lay out the three appliquéd star blocks and the two border pairs in a row. Sew together the pieces to make the top border unit. Press the seam allowances in one direction.

Diagram 1

4. Sew the top border unit to the top edge of the appliquéd center block. Press the seam allowances toward the border.

5. Sew together the assorted print 1½" squares in pairs. Press the seam allowances in one direction. Then join two pairs to make a Four-Patch unit (see Diagram 2). Repeat to make a total of four Four-Patch units.

Diagram 2

6. Referring to Diagram 3 for placement, lay out the five assorted print 2½" squares and the four Four-Patch units. Sew together the pieces to make the pieced border unit. Press the seam allowances toward the 2½" squares.

Diagram 3

7. Sew the pieced border unit to the bottom edge of the center block to complete the quilt top.

complete the quilt

1. Layer the quilt top, batting, and backing according to the instructions in Quilting Basics, which begins on *page 94*. Quilt as desired.

2. Use the black plaid 2½"-wide bias strips to bind the quilt according to the instructions in Quilting Basics.

COLOR OPTION
Simply choosing floral fabrics for this small quilt gives it a quick change of style. The light, airy tones of the quilt would look great in a blue-and-yellow kitchen.

Appliqué Placement Diagram

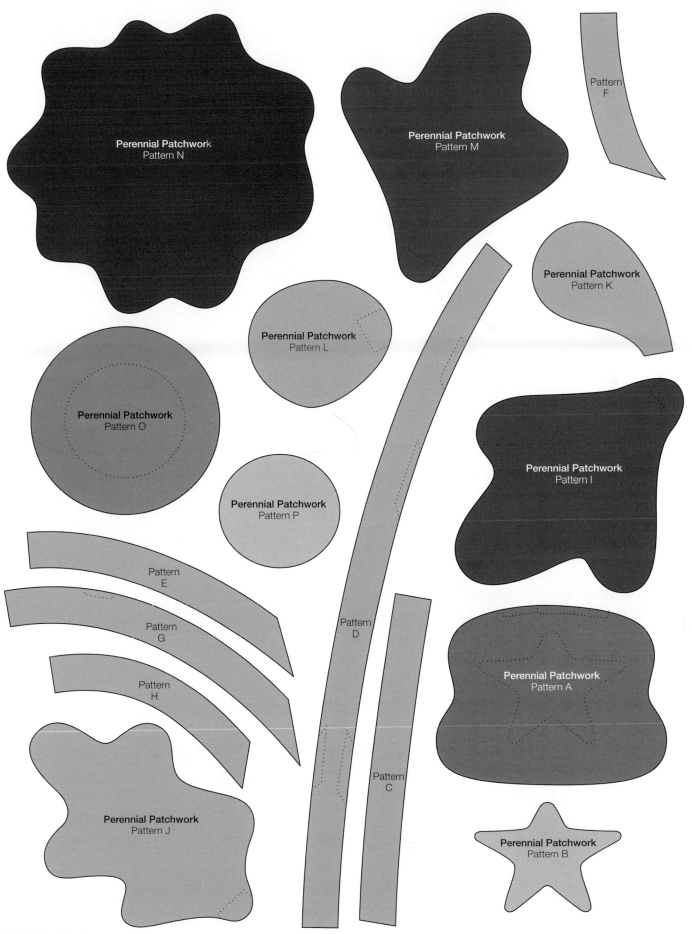

Perennial Patchwork
Pattern N

Perennial Patchwork
Pattern M

Pattern
F

Perennial Patchwork
Pattern K

Perennial Patchwork
Pattern L

Perennial Patchwork
Pattern O

Perennial Patchwork
Pattern I

Perennial Patchwork
Pattern P

Pattern
E

Pattern
G

Pattern
H

Pattern
D

Perennial Patchwork
Pattern A

Pattern
C

Perennial Patchwork
Pattern J

Perennial Patchwork
Pattern B

Full-Size Patterns

sun-ripened
berries

Celebrate fields filled with cranberries, blueberries,
and colorful wildflowers with two coordinating small
quilts embellished with random hand-quilting.

Designer: Carol Armstrong   Photographer: Marcia Cameron

materials for both quilts

¾ yard of muslin for appliqué foundations and backings

¼ yard of solid red for cranberry appliqués and binding

¼ yard of solid blue for blueberry appliqués and binding

Scraps of solid yellow, gold, light green, green, and beige for appliqués

Embroidery floss: green, black, cream, and yellow

2—12×14" pieces of quilt batting

Water-soluble fabric marker

FINISHED QUILT TOP: 10×12½"

Quantities specified for 44/45"-wide, 100% cotton fabrics. All measurements include a ¼" seam allowance. Sew with right sides together unless otherwise stated.

cut the fabrics

To make the best use of your fabrics, cut the pieces in the order that follows. The patterns are on *pages 42–43*. To make templates of the patterns, follow the instructions in Appliqué Primer, which begins on *page 84*. Because no two pieces are alike, you'll want to create a template for each pattern.

When cutting out appliqué pieces, add a ³⁄₁₆" seam allowance.

From muslin, cut:
● 4—12×14" rectangles for appliqué foundations and backing

From solid red, cut:
● 2—2½×42" binding strips
● 21 different cranberry appliqués

From solid blue, cut:
● 2—2½×42" binding strips
● 21 different blueberry appliqués

From solid yellow and solid gold, cut:
● 60 different sunflower petal appliqués

From solid light green, cut:
● 14 different sunflower leaf appliqués

From solid green, cut:
● 12 different blueberry leaf appliqués
● 25 different cranberry leaf appliqués

From solid beige, cut:
● 6 different sunflower center appliqués

prepare the appliqué foundations

1. Place the patterns on a light table or glass window and secure in place. Cover the Full-size Cranberry Pattern with a muslin 12×14" foundation. Transfer the Cranberry Pattern to the fabric. Repeat with the Full-size Blueberry Pattern and the remaining muslin 12×14" foundation.

2. Pin the appliqué pieces in place on each foundation.

3. Using threads in colors that match the fabrics, appliqué each piece to the foundations, turning the edges under with your needle as you work. You do not need to turn under edges that will be overlapped by other pieces. In the case of extremely small pieces, you may need to trim away part of the seam allowance. Begin with the pieces on the bottom and work up. (The numbers on the patterns indicate the appliquéing sequence.) Designer Carol Armstrong suggests appliquéing with a blind stitch or tack stitch.

4. Using two strands of green embroidery floss, stem-stitch all of the stems. (For specific instructions on stem-stitching, see Embroidery Stitches on *page 93*.) To make the sunflower stems look thicker, Carol stem-stitched two rows close together.

5. Using two strands of yellow embroidery floss, add three to five French knots to the center of each sunflower. (For specific instructions on French knots, see Embroidery Stitches.)

6. Using two strands of black embroidery floss, take a single stitch, about ⅛" to ¼" long, at the bottom of each red cranberry appliqué for a stem.

7. Using one strand of cream embroidery floss, stem-stitch a small crescent shape of two to three stitches on each blueberry appliqué.

8. Remove any remaining quilt markings that may show; press the appliquéd foundations from the back on a soft surface, such as a folded towel.

9. Trim the appliquéd foundations to measure 10½×13", including the seam allowances. Carol cut the foundations so the appliqué designs were approximately 2½" from the top edge, 1½" from the bottom edge, and 1½" from each side edge.

complete the quilts

1. Layer the quilt tops, battings, and backings according to the instructions in Quilting Basics, which begins on *page 94*.

2. Quilt as desired. Carol first hand-quilted a random scattering of leaves in the backgrounds. Then she hand-quilted straight lines in multiple directions all over, but not through the appliqués or quilted leaves. She used masking tape to create straight edges for quilting. To make her quilting design interesting, she avoided quilting any lines parallel with either the top or side edges of the quilt top.

3. Use either the solid red or solid blue 2½×42" strips to bind the quilts according to the instructions in Quilting Basics.

Full-Size Cranberry Pattern

Full-Size Blueberry Pattern

tomato soup
and bay leaves

Combine a variety of red decorator prints to create this delightful two-block quilt embellished with sprigs of appliquéd bay leaves.

Designer: Carol Armstrong Photographer: Marcia Cameron

materials

- 1¾ yards of light red plaid for blocks
- 1¾ yards of dark red plaid for blocks
- 1¼ yards of red stripe for blocks
- 1¼ yards of large red print for blocks
- ⅔ yard of red toile for blocks
- ⅛ yard of small red print for border cornerstones
- 1⅛ yards of light green print for leaf appliqués
- ⅔ yard of green plaid for border
- ⅞ yard of dark green print for binding
- 5⅛ yards of backing fabric
- 91×105" of quilt batting
- 10 skeins of light green embroidery floss
- 6 skeins of dark red embroidery floss

FINISHED QUILT TOP: 85×98½"
FINISHED BLOCK: 13½" square

Quantities specified are for 58/60"-wide decorator fabric. All measurements include a ¼" seam allowance. Sew with right sides together unless otherwise stated.

cut the fabrics

To make the best use of your fabrics, cut the pieces in the order that follows. The appliqué pattern is on *page 46*. To make a template of the pattern, follow the instructions in Appliqué Primer, which begins on *page 84*.

From light red plaid, cut:
- 10—5⅜×56" strips

From dark red plaid, cut:
- 10—5⅜×56" strips

From red stripe, cut:
- 84—5" squares

From large red print, cut:
- 84—5" squares

From red toile, cut:
- 42—5" squares

From small red print, cut:
- 4—2½" squares

From light green print, cut:
- 72—5" squares

From green plaid, cut:
- 7—2½×56" strips for border

From dark green print, cut:
- 7—4×56" binding strips

1. Layer a light red plaid 5⅜×56" strip and a dark red plaid 5⅜×56" strip; press to temporarily hold the strips together. Cut the layered strips into nine layered 5⅜" squares (see Diagram 1).

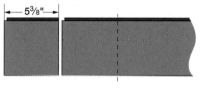
Diagram 1

2. Referring to Diagram 2, cut a pair of layered 5⅜" squares in half diagonally to make two pairs of layered triangles. Sew together each pair of layered triangles to make two triangle-squares. Press the seam allowances toward the dark red plaid triangles. Each pieced triangle-square should measure 5" square, including the seam allowances. Repeat with the remaining pairs of layered squares to make a total of 18 triangle-squares.

Diagram 2

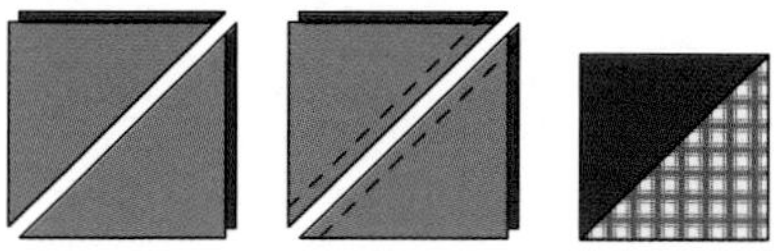

3. Repeat steps 1 and 2 with the remaining light red plaid and dark red plaid 5⅜×56" strips to make a total of 168 triangle-squares.

4. Referring to Diagram 3 for placement, sew together four triangle-squares, four red stripe 5" squares, and one red toile 5" square in three rows (position the stripes so they all run in the same direction). Press the seam allowances toward the red stripe squares. Sew together the rows to make a Block A. Press the seam allowances in one direction. Pieced Block A should measure 14" square, including the seam allowances. Repeat to make a total of 21 of Block A.

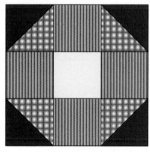
Diagram 3

5. Referring to Diagram 4 on *page 46*, sew together four triangle-squares, four large red print 5" squares, and one red toile 5" square in three rows. Press the seam allowances toward the large red print squares. Sew together the rows to make a Block B. Press the seam allowances in one direction. Pieced Block B should measure 14" square, including the seam allowances. Repeat to make a total of 21 of Block B.

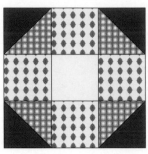

Diagram 4

6. Using six strands of dark red embroidery floss, whipstitch around the edges of the center toile square of each Block A and B and make a cross-stitch at each corner (see Diagram 5).

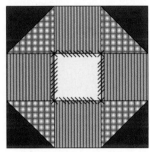

Diagram 5

assemble the quilt center

1. Referring to the photograph *opposite* for placement, lay out all the pieced blocks in seven horizontal rows, alternating A and B blocks.

2. Sew together the blocks in each row. Press the seam allowances toward Block A. Then join the rows to make the quilt center. Press the seam allowances in one direction. The pieced quilt center should measure 81½×95", including the seam allowances.

appliqué the quilt center

1. Fold a light green print 5" square in half with right sides together and use a pencil to trace the pattern once on the wrong side. Do not cut out the traced pattern. Repeat with the remaining light green print 5" squares.

2. Machine-stitch around each traced pattern on the traced lines, stitching through both fabric layers. Cut out the leaf shapes ⅛" outside the stitched lines. Cut a small slit through one layer of each leaf shape (see Diagram 6). Turn each leaf right side out and press.

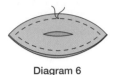

Diagram 6

3. Referring to the photograph *opposite*, pin four leaves to each of the 18 red plaid squares that were formed when the blocks were joined into the quilt center. Each leaf will cover a seam.

4. Using thread in a color that matches the fabric, appliqué the leaves in place.

add the borders

1. Cut and piece the green plaid 2½×56" strips to make the following:
● 2—2½×95" border strips
● 2—2½×81½" border strips

2. Sew the short green plaid border strips to the top and bottom edges of the pieced quilt center. Press the seam allowances toward the green plaid border.

3. Sew a small red print 2½" square to each end of the long green plaid border strips to make two side border units. Press the seam allowances toward the green plaid strips. Join the border units to the side edges of the pieced quilt center to complete the quilt top. Press the seam allowances toward the green print border.

complete the quilt

1. Layer the quilt top, batting, and backing according to the instructions in Quilting Basics, which begins on *page 94*.

2. Using six strands of green embroidery floss, hand-quilt in an octagon shape on each pieced block (see Diagram 7, *above right*).

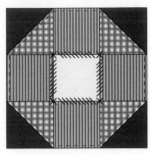

Diagram 7

3. Using a ¾" seam allowance, bind the quilt with the dark green print 4×56" strips according to the instructions in Quilting Basics.

Tomato Soup and Bay Leaves
Leaf Pattern

Full-Size Pattern

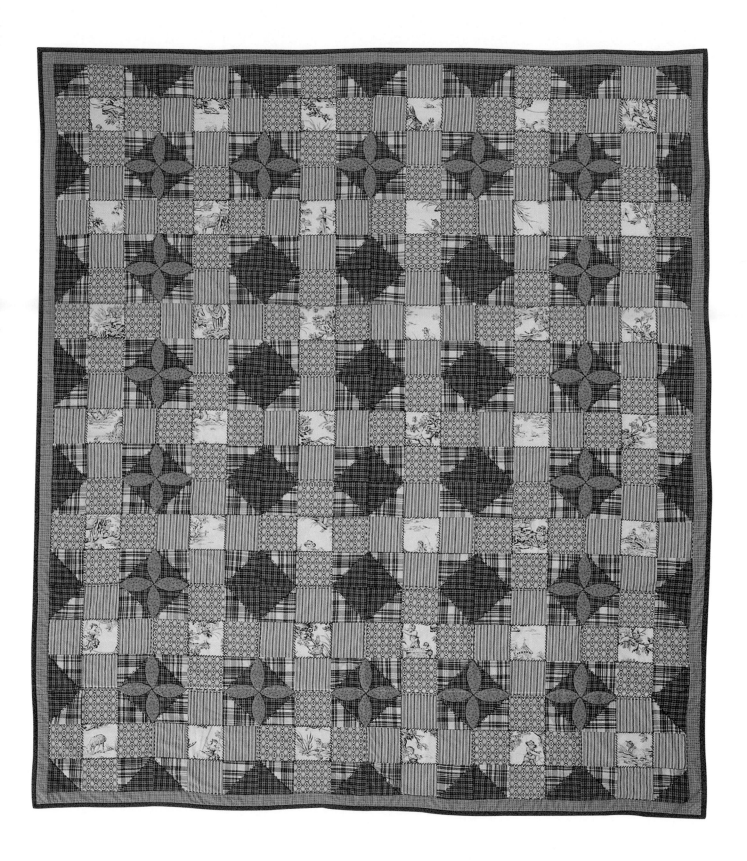

wool appliqué

Tactile and versatile, felted wool is a favorite of appliqué enthusiasts. With no ends to turn under and no stitching that needs to hide, you'll love showing off your favorite embroidery stitches on these projects.

heaven
and earth

This folk art wall hanging of wool uses simple appliqué shapes. Wool can be found today in nearly every type of fabric store, including quilt shops.

Designer: Marty Freed   Photographer: Perry Struse

materials

1 yard of black-and-white print wool for appliqué foundation, border, and border corners

¾ yard of solid black wool for border

½ yard of solid turquoise felted wool for appliqués and border

⅞ yard of solid purple felted wool for appliqués and border

⅜ yard of solid green felted wool for appliqués

¼ yard of solid red felted wool for appliqués and border

⅛ yard of solid white felted wool for appliqués and border

¼ yard of solid burgundy felted wool for appliqués and border corners

¼ yard *each* of solid gold, and solid bright blue felted wool for appliqués

⅛ yard *each* of solid brown and plaid felted wool for appliqués

3¼ yards of solid black flannel for backing and binding

58×62" of quilt batting

Perle cotton thread: gold, red, and black

FINISHED QUILT TOP: 51½×55½"

Quantities specified for 44/45"-wide, 100% wool or cotton fabrics. All measurements include a ¼" seam allowance. Sew with right sides together unless otherwise stated.

cut the fabrics

To make the best use of your fabrics, cut the pieces in the order that follows. Cut the appliqué shapes to their finished sizes. No seam allowances are necessary because felted wool appliqués can be stitched in place without having to turn under the edges.

The patterns begin on *page 51*. To make templates of the patterns, follow the instructions in Appliqué Primer, which begins on *page 84*.

From black-and-white print wool, cut:
● 2—3×42" inner border strips
● 2—3×33" inner border strips
● 1—22×26" rectangle for appliqué foundation
● 4—4⅜" squares

From solid black wool, cut:
● 2—6×33" strips for woven border
● 2—6×26" strips for woven border

From solid turquoise wool, cut:
● 2—2×45" middle border strips
● 2—2×38" middle border strips
● 1 of Pattern A
● 2 of Pattern F

From solid purple wool, cut:
● 2—6×45" outer border strips
● 2—6×41" outer border strips
● 1 of Pattern I

From solid green wool, cut:
● 1 *each* of patterns D, E, and E reversed
● 2 *each* of patterns H, M, CC, DD, and FF
● 12 of Pattern P

From solid red wool, cut:
● 4—1×27" strips for woven border
● 2 *each* of patterns G, N, and Q
● 1 *each* of patterns C, Z, and BB
● 3 of Pattern AA

From solid white wool, cut:
● 2—1×27" strips for woven border
● 4 of Pattern Q
● 2 of Pattern S
● 1 *each* of patterns V and V reversed

From solid burgundy wool, cut:
● 4—5⅛" squares, cutting each diagonally twice in an X for a total of 16 triangles
● 1 *each* of patterns J and J reversed

From solid gold wool, cut:
● 1 *each* of patterns B, K, Y, and AA
● 12 of Pattern O
● 5 of Pattern X
● 3 of Pattern Z

From solid bright blue wool, cut:
● 1 *each* of patterns L, L reversed, T, T reversed, U, and U reversed
● 3 of Pattern R

From solid brown wool, cut:
● 3 of Pattern S
● 2 of Pattern W
● 4 of Pattern EE

From plaid wool, cut:
● 4 of Pattern N
● 2 of Pattern R

From solid black flannel, cut:
● 6—2½×42" binding strips

appliqué the center section

1. Referring to the photograph on *page 49* for placement, arrange appliqué pieces A through L on the black-and-white print 22×26" appliqué foundation.

2. Using three strands of gold perle cotton thread, blanket-stitch around each piece to make the center section. (For specific instructions on blanket-stitching, see Embroidery Stitches on *page 93*.)

Using two strands of gold perle cotton thread, make three French knots in the center of each red G circle. (For specific instructions on French knots, see Quilting Basics.)

add the woven border

1. In each solid black 6×26" border strip, cut twelve 3"-wide slits approximately 2" apart, starting 2" from one end (see Diagram 1 *below left*). Weave two solid red 1×27"strips and one solid white 1×27" strip through the slits in each black strip (see Diagram 2 *below right*). Pin at each end. Make sure the ends are secure in the seam allowance.

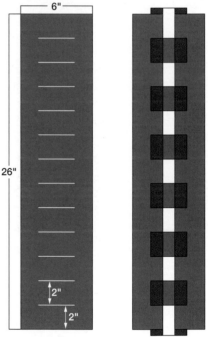

Diagram 1   Diagram 2

2. Join the woven border strips to the side edges of the appliquéd center section. Press the seam allowances toward the woven border. Sew the solid black 6×33" border strips to the top and bottom edges of the appliquéd center section to complete the quilt center. Press the seam allowances toward the black border. The pieced quilt center should measure 33×37", including the seam allowances.

3. Referring to the photograph on *page 49* for placement, arrange appliqué pieces M through P on the top and bottom solid black border strips.

4. Using three strands of gold perle cotton thread, blanket-stitch around each piece. Using two strands of black perle cotton thread, satin-stitch the center of each gold O circle (see Satin Stitch diagram).

Satin Stitch

add the borders

1. Sew the black-and-white print 3×33" inner border strips to the top and bottom edges of the quilt center. Then add the black-and-white print 3×42" inner border strip to the side edges of the quilt center. Press the seam allowances toward the black-and-white print border.

2. Sew the solid turquoise 2×38" middle border strips to the top and bottom edges of the quilt center. Then add the solid turquoise 2×45" middle border strips to the side edges of the quilt center. Press the seam allowances toward the turquoise border.

3. Referring to Diagram 3, *above right,* sew two solid burgundy triangles to opposite edges of a black-and-white print 4⅜" square. Press the seam allowances toward the triangles. Add the solid burgundy triangles to the square's remaining raw edges in the same manner to make a border block; press. The pieced border block should measure 6" square, including the seam allowances. Repeat to make a total of four border blocks.

Diagram 3

4. Sew the solid purple 6×41" outer border strips to the top and bottom edges of the quilt center. Press the seam allowances toward the purple border.

5. Sew a border block to each end of the solid purple 6×45" outer border strips. Press the seam allowances toward the solid purple strips. Sew the pieced border strips to the side edges of the quilt center to complete the quilt top. Press the seam allowances toward the solid purple border.

6. Referring to the photograph on *page 49* for placement, arrange the remaining appliqué pieces (Q through FF) on the solid purple borders.

7. Using three strands of gold or black perle cotton thread, blanket-stitch around each appliqué piece.

complete the quilt

1. Layer the quilt top, batting, and backing according to the instructions in Quilting Basics, which begins on *page 94.*

2. Quilt as desired. The black-and-white print areas of this quilt were quilted in a meandering pattern.

3. Use the solid black flannel 2½×42" strips to bind the quilt according to the instructions in Quilting Basics.

Heaven and Earth
Pattern K

Heaven and Earth
Pattern G

Heaven and Earth
Pattern O

Heaven and Earth
Pattern BB

Heaven and Earth
Pattern C

Heaven and Earth
Pattern B

Full-Size Patterns

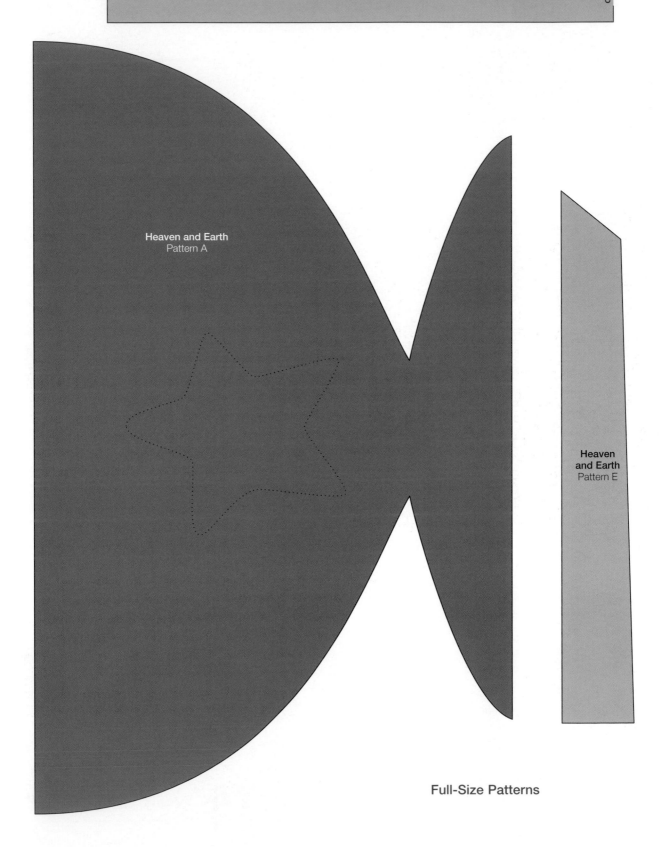

Heaven and Earth
Pattern D

center

Heaven and Earth
Pattern A

Heaven and Earth
Pattern E

Full-Size Patterns

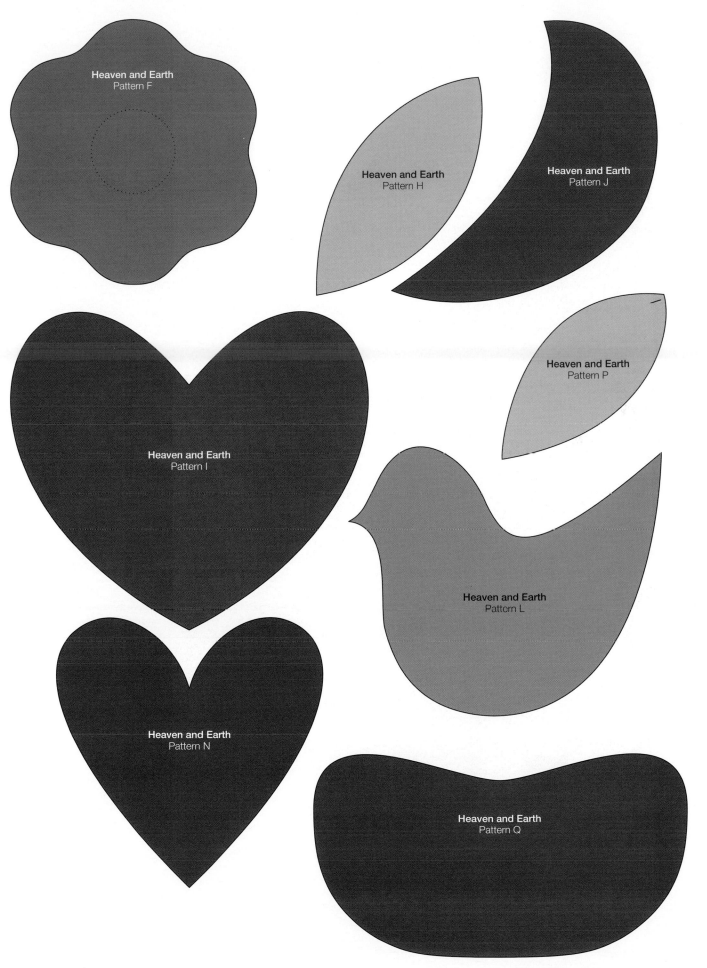

Heaven and Earth
Pattern F

Heaven and Earth
Pattern H

Heaven and Earth
Pattern J

Heaven and Earth
Pattern P

Heaven and Earth
Pattern I

Heaven and Earth
Pattern L

Heaven and Earth
Pattern N

Heaven and Earth
Pattern Q

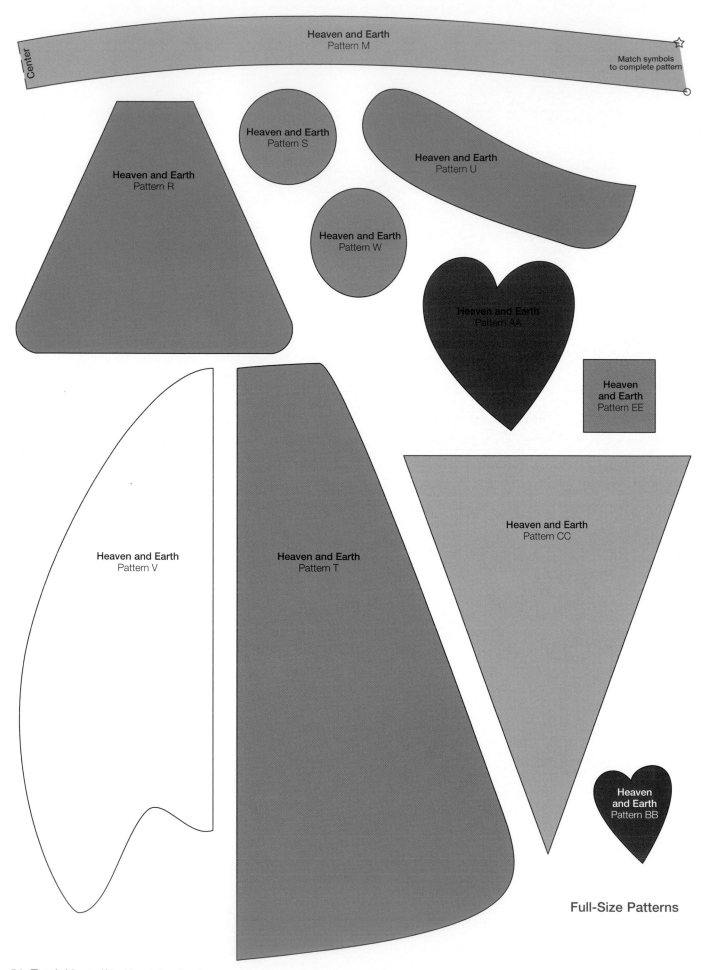

Heaven and Earth
Pattern M

Center

Match symbols
to complete pattern

Heaven and Earth
Pattern S

Heaven and Earth
Pattern U

Heaven and Earth
Pattern R

Heaven and Earth
Pattern W

Heaven and Earth
Pattern AA

Heaven
and Earth
Pattern EE

Heaven and Earth
Pattern V

Heaven and Earth
Pattern T

Heaven and Earth
Pattern CC

Heaven
and Earth
Pattern BB

Full-Size Patterns

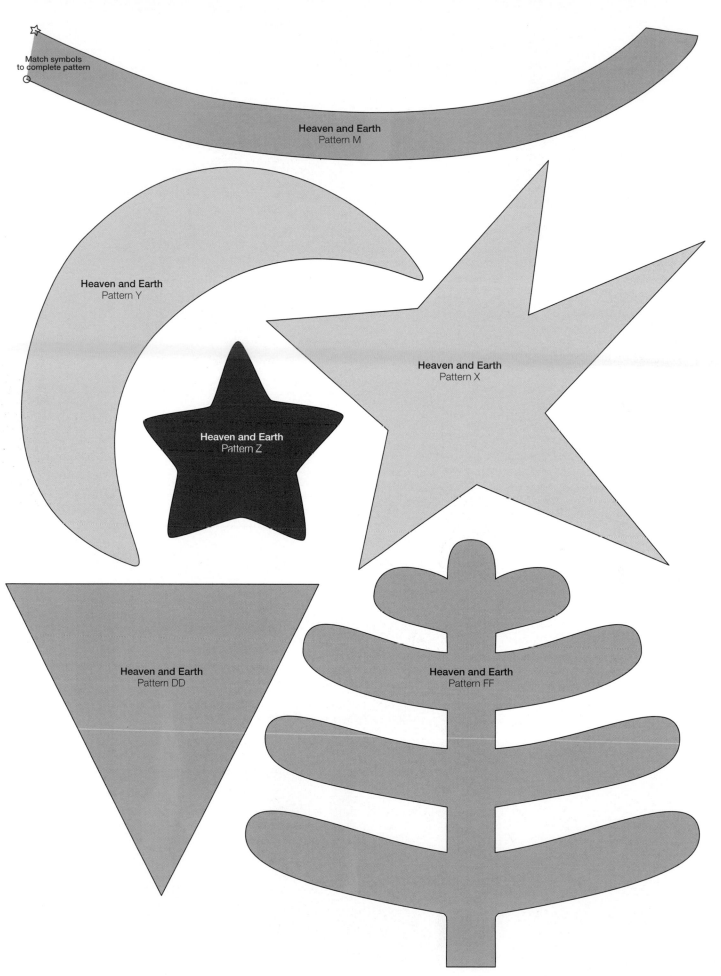

Match symbols
to complete pattern

Heaven and Earth
Pattern M

Heaven and Earth
Pattern Y

Heaven and Earth
Pattern Z

Heaven and Earth
Pattern X

Heaven and Earth
Pattern DD

Heaven and Earth
Pattern FF

appliquéd coat

Stitching the long, winding vine on this denim coat is easy when you use fusible web to secure the pieces.

Designer: Peggy Kotek
Photographer: Perry Struse

materials

Scraps of assorted red and light green felted wool
⅛ yard of dark green felted wool
Embroidery floss: red and green
Purchased denim coat
Lightweight fusible web

about the wool

Felted wool is a favorite of quilters because its edges won't unravel when cut. The wools used in this project were hand-dyed for a mottled appearance.

To felt wool, machine-wash it in warm water with a small amount of detergent and machine-dry. If you choose to use wool from a piece of clothing, cut it apart and remove the seams before you felt it so it can shrink freely and evenly.

cut the fabrics

To make the best use of your fabrics, cut the pieces in the order that follows.

To use fusible web for appliquéing, as was done in this project, complete the following steps.

1. Lay the fusible web, paper side up, over the patterns. Use a pencil to trace each pattern the number of times indicated, leaving a ½" space between tracings. Cut out each piece roughly ¼" outside the traced lines.

2. Following the manufacturer's instructions, press the fusible-web shapes onto the wrong sides of the designated fabrics; let cool. Cut out the fabric shapes on the drawn lines. Peel off the paper backings.

From assorted red wool, cut:
● 23 of Pattern B
From assorted light green wool, cut:
● 24—⅜×1¼" strips for stem appliqués
● 15 of Pattern A
From dark green wool, cut:
● ⅜"-wide strips, enough to make the following lengths for vine appliqués: 1½", 2", 12", 14", and 24"

appliqué the coat

1. Referring to the photograph *opposite*, position the vine and stem appliqué strips on the coat. Baste in place. Then position the prepared appliqué pieces on the coat, working from the bottom layer to the top. Fuse in place.

2. Using color-coordinated embroidery threads, blanket-stitch around each appliqué piece. (For specific instructions on blanket stitch, see Embroidery Stitches on *page 93*.)

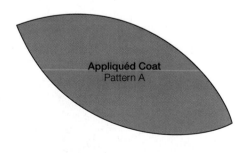

Appliquéd Coat
Pattern A

Appliquéd Coat
Pattern B

Full-Size Patterns

Surprise a special grandmother or mom with this touching wall hanging. A handprint representing every grandchild blooms in the center and around the borders.

Designer: Heidi Kaisand
Photographer: Perry Struse

grandmother's
handprint

materials

24x28" rectangle of bright green felted wool for appliqué foundation

22—5" squares of felted wool in assorted purple, blue, and raspberry for appliqués

2—5" squares of yellow felted wool for appliqués

1—5" square of pink felted wool for appliqués

⅛ yard of dark blue felted wool for inner border

¼ yard of dark purple felted wool for outer border

24x28" rectangle of purple print cotton for backing

Perle cotton thread in matching colors, plus assorted greens

FINISHED WALL HANGING: 24×28"

cut the fabrics

To make the best use of your fabrics, cut the pieces in the order that follows. To make templates of the patterns, follow the instructions in Appliqué Primer, which begins on *page 84*. Remember: Do not add any seam allowances when cutting out appliqué shapes from felted wool.

From assorted purple and blue wool, cut:
● 8 of Pattern A
● 9 of Pattern A reversed
● 5 of Pattern F
● 1 of Pattern E

From assorted raspberry wool, cut:
● 3 of Pattern A
● 2 of Pattern A reversed
● 5 of Pattern G
● 1 of Pattern C

From yellow wool, cut:
● 1 of Pattern A
● 5 of Pattern D

From pink wool, cut:
● 4 of Pattern B

From dark blue wool, cut:
● 2—½×16" border strips
● 2—½×15" border strips

From dark purple wool, cut:
● 2—1¼×28" binding strips
● 2—1¼×24" binding strips

appliqué and embroider the foundation

1. Referring to the photograph *opposite* for placement, in the center of the bright green 24×28" appliqué foundation position the dark blue ½×16" border strips on each side and the dark blue ½×15" border strips on the top and bottom edges to make a rectangle; pin in place. Then position the appliqué pieces as desired. Once you're pleased with the arrangement, pin the pieces in place.

2. Use one strand of matching perle cotton to stitch the inner border and appliqué pieces in place with a blanket stitch, running stitch, or other embroidery stitch (for specific instructions, see *page 93*).

3. Use one strand of green perle cotton and a decorative embroidery stitch to add stems to each flower and handprint inside the inner border to complete the appliqué.

4. Steam press the appliquéd foundation on the wrong side only to prevent flattening the appliqués and stitching.

complete the quilt

1. With wrong sides together, layer the appliquéd foundation and the purple print cotton 24×28" rectangle. Pin or baste the layers together. Quilt as desired through all layers.

2. Use the dark purple 1¼×28" strips to bind each side edge of the quilt by wrapping each strip over an edge and sewing through all layers with a running stitch and one strand of matching perle cotton. Repeat with the dark purple 1¼×24" binding strips and the top and bottom edges of the quilt.

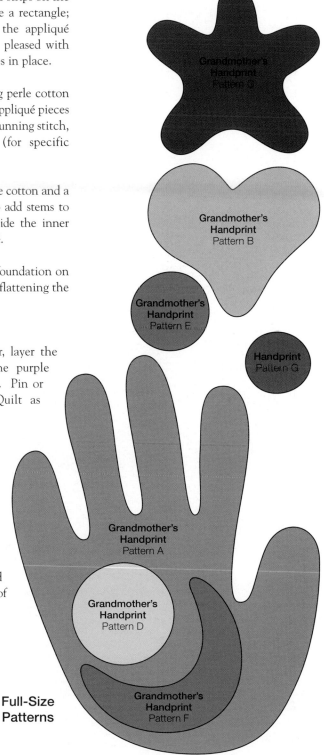

Grandmother's Handprint Pattern C

Grandmother's Handprint Pattern B

Grandmother's Handprint Pattern E

Handprint Pattern G

Grandmother's Handprint Pattern A

Grandmother's Handprint Pattern D

Grandmother's Handprint Pattern F

Full-Size Patterns

wool
wall hanging

Try your hand at an array of embroidery stitches to appliqué these hand-dyed felted wool flowers.

Designer: Roseann Kermes
Photographer: Perry Struse

materials

Scraps of assorted blue, red, purple, pink, orange, and gold felted wools for flower and triangle appliqués

⅝ yard of sage green felted wool for appliqué foundation

⅜ yard of black felted wool for appliqué foundation, triangle appliqués, and binding

⅓ yard of yellow check felted wool for appliqué foundations

⅛ yard total of assorted dark green felted wools for leaf and stem appliqués

1¼ yards of homespun cotton for backing

2 yards of lightweight fusible web

Embroidery floss: gold, black, and green

Freezer paper

FINISHED WALL HANGING: 43×21"

about the wool

Felted wool is a favorite of quilters because its edges won't ravel when cut. The wools used in this project were hand-dyed for a mottled appearance.

To felt wool, machine-wash it in warm-water with a small amount of detergent and machine-dry. If you choose to use wool from a piece of clothing, cut it apart and remove the seams before you felt it so it can shrink freely.

cut the fabrics

To make the best use of your fabrics, cut the pieces in the order that follows. The patterns are on *page 63*. To use freezer-paper templates for cutting the appliqué shapes, as was done in this project, complete the following steps.

1. Place the patterns on a light box and position the freezer paper, shiny side down, over the patterns (see Photo 1). With a pencil, trace the patterns the number of times specified, leaving ½" between tracings. Cut out the freezer-paper shapes about ¼" outside the traced lines.

2. Press the freezer-paper shapes onto the right sides of the designated fabrics (see Photo 2); let cool.

3. Cut out the fabric shapes along the solid traced lines, cutting the fabric edges cleanly and smoothly; peel off the freezer paper (see Photo 3).

From assorted blue, red, purple, pink, orange, and gold wool, cut:
- 17 *each* of patterns A and B
- 13—1" squares

From sage green wool, cut:
- 1—19×43" rectangle for appliqué foundation

From black wool, cut:
- 1—1×43" binding strip
- 1—11" square for appliqué foundation
- 7—3" squares, cutting each in half diagonally for a total of 14 triangle appliqués (you'll have 1 leftover triangle)

From yellow checked wool, cut:
- 2—10" squares for appliqué foundations

From assorted dark green wools, cut:
- 6 of Pattern C
- 14 of Pattern D
- 7 of Pattern E
- 3 *each* of patterns F and G

From homespun, cut:
- 1—19×43" rectangle for backing
- 7—3" squares, cutting each in half diagonally for a total of 14 triangles (you'll have 1 leftover triangle)

From fusible web, cut:
- 1—19×43" rectangle
- 7—3" squares, cutting each in half diagonally for a total of 14 triangles (you'll have 1 leftover triangle)

appliqué the flower blocks

1. Referring to Photo 4, the photograph *opposite*, and the Block Appliqué Placement Diagram on *page 63*, position the appliqué shapes on the foundations, layering as needed from bottom to top. Baste the leaf, stem, and flower appliqué pieces onto the yellow check 10" squares and the black 11" square.

2. Using matching thread, hand-stitch the appliqués in place. Using two strands of green embroidery floss, randomly couch the stems so the wool shows through.

To couch, refer to the diagram on *page 62*. First pull your needle up at A. Insert the needle back into the fabric at B and come up again at C. Continue in this manner along each stem.

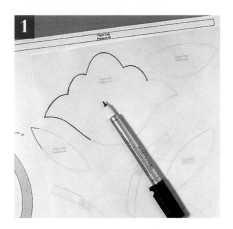

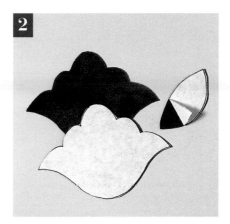

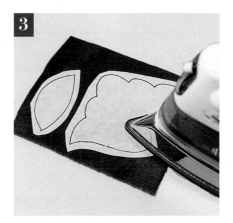

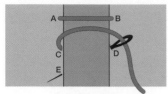
Couching Stitch

3. Stitch the leaves down their centers using a running stitch. (For specific instructions on the running stitch, see Embroidery Stitches on page 93.)

4. Using two strands of gold embroidery floss, cross-stitch along the top edge of the flower bases.

   To cross-stitch, refer to the diagram at *right*. Pull your needle up at A, then push it down at B. Bring your needle up at C, cross over the first stitch, and push your needle down at D to form an X.

Cross-Stitch

appliqué the background
1. Referring to the Appliqué Placement Diagram *opposite,* position the three appliquéd squares on the sage green 19×43" rectangle and pin in place. Using two strands of black embroidery floss, blanket-stitch the yellow check appliquéd squares in place. (For specific instruction on the blanket stitch, see Embroidery Stitches.)

2. Using two strands of gold embroidery floss, blanket-stitch the black flower block in place.

3. Referring to the Appliqué Placement Diagram, pin the remaining appliqué pieces along the bottom edge of the sage green rectangle. Hand-stitch in place as before.

assemble the quilt
1. Following the manufacturer's instructions, fuse the fusible-web 19×43" rectangle to the wrong side of the homespun 19×43" rectangle; remove the paper backing. Layer the appliquéd rectangle and the homespun; fuse together. Using three strands of black embroidery floss, blanket-stitch together the two side edges and the bottom edges.

2. Referring to the photograph *above* and using two strands of black embroidery floss, quilt ¼" from the edges of the appliquéd squares.

complete the quilt
1. Fold the black wool 1×43" strip in half lengthwise; press. Open up the strip and place the top edge of the quilt right side up along the fold line. Fold the strip over the edge; pin to the front of the quilt to form the binding. Using one strand of black embroidery floss, whipstitch the front edge of the strip to the quilt. Repeat with the back edge.

2. To make the triangle appliqués, place an assorted wool 1" square on each black triangle appliqué so the straight edges are ¼" from the bottom edges and the points are aligned (see Triangle Appliqué Diagram, *above right*). Using one strand of gold

embroidery floss, whipstitch the squares in place. Using two strands of gold embroidery floss, make a cross-stitch in the center of each square.

3. Place a fusible-web triangle on the back of an appliquéd triangle; fuse in place. Remove the paper backing. Fuse an appliquéd triangle to each homespun triangle. Using two strands of gold embroidery floss, blanket-stitch around the edges of the triangles.

Triangle Appliqué Diagram

4. Pin an appliquéd triangle to the center bottom edge of the wall hanging so the raw edges are touching. Overlap the remaining triangles evenly along the wall hanging edge. Using one strand of black embroidery floss, whipstitch each triangle in place. Using a pressing cloth, carefully steam-press. Allow to dry completely.

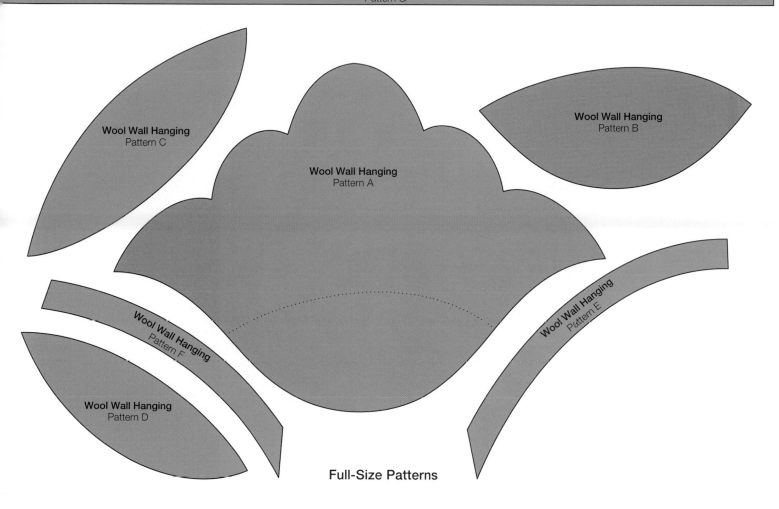

Wool Wall Hanging
Pattern G

Wool Wall Hanging
Pattern C

Wool Wall Hanging
Pattern A

Wool Wall Hanging
Pattern B

Wool Wall Hanging
Pattern F

Wool Wall Hanging
Pattern E

Wool Wall Hanging
Pattern D

Full-Size Patterns

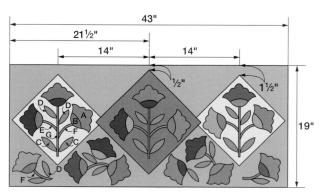

Appliqué Placement Diagram

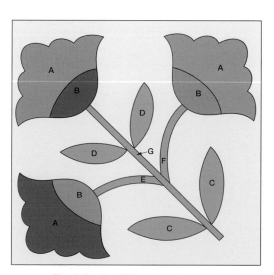

Block Appliqué Placement Diagram

fused
and
hand-stitched
appliqué

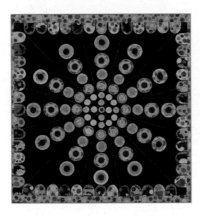 

Discover a shortcut
that allows even the
busiest quilters to
enjoy appliqué.
Affix cutout shapes
with fusible web to
keep the pieces
from shifting before
you take a stitch,
then embellish the
shapes with your
own embroidery.

starburst
penny rug

Penny rugs
were once a
mainstay on
Early American
tabletops.
This cheerful
contemporary
variation
contrasts a
black
background
with stacks
of round
appliqués in
playful colors.

Designer: Janet Carija Brandt
Photographer: Perry Struse

materials

- 3—18×22" pieces (fat quarters) of assorted green prints for penny appliqués, petals, and inner border
- 3—18×22" pieces (fat quarters) of assorted yellow prints for penny appliqués, petals, inner border,and binding
- 1½ yards of black print for appliqué foundation and outer border
- 1—18×22" piece (fat quarter) of red print for penny appliqués and petals
- 1¼ yards of backing fabric
- 44" square of quilt batting
- 1 yard of lightweight fusible web
- Embroidery floss in coordinating colors

FINISHED QUILT TOP: 37½" square

Quantities specified for 44/45"-wide, 100% cotton fabrics. All measurements include a ¼" seam allowance. Sew with right sides together unless otherwise indicated.

designer notes

In making this penny rug, designer Janet Carija Brandt utilized lightweight fusible web only along the outer edges of the cotton appliqué pieces. This stabilized the edges so they didn't fray or need to be turned under. It also reduced the bulk usually associated with using fusible web, giving the completed quilt a softer hand than traditional fused-appliqué projects.

cut the fabrics

To make the best use of your fabrics, cut the pieces in the order that follows. The patterns are shown *opposite*. To use fusible web for appliquéing, as was done in this project, complete the following steps.

1. Lay the fusible web, paper side up, over the patterns. Use a pencil to trace each pattern the number of times indicated, leaving a ½" space between tracings. Cut out each piece roughly ¼" outside the traced lines. Cut ⅛" inside the traced lines of each piece and discard the centers.

2. Following the manufacturer's instructions, press the fusible-web shapes onto the wrong sides of the designated fabrics; let cool. Cut

out the fabric shapes on the drawn lines. Peel off the paper backing.

From assorted green prints, cut:
- 4—2½×22" binding strips
- 6—2×22" binding strips
- 84 of Pattern E
- 12 *each* of patterns B and D
- 24 of Pattern C

From assorted yellow prints, cut:
- 4—2½×22" binding strips
- 84 of Pattern E
- 29 of Pattern B
- 24 of Pattern C
- 12 of Pattern D

From black print, cut:
- 1—30½" square for appliqué foundation
- 2—2¾×38" outer border strips
- 2—2¾×33½" outer border strips
- 28 of Pattern E

From red print, cut:
- 28 of Pattern E
- 24 of Pattern B
- 1 of Pattern A

appliqué the quilt center

1. To create placement guidelines, fold the black print 30½" square on the diagonals and press. Unfold and use a quilter's pencil to lightly mark crease lines and divide each quarter into three sections.

2. Referring to the photograph *below* for placement, lay out appliqué pieces A through D, using the guidelines to keep the rows straight. When pleased with the placement of the appliqués, fuse them in place.

3. Using two strands of embroidery floss, blanket-stitch around each piece to complete the quilt center.

To blanket-stitch, pull the needle up at A (see Blanket Stitch Diagram *opposite*), form a reverse L shape with the floss, and hold the angle of the L shape in place with your thumb. Push the needle down at B and come up at C to secure the stitch. Continue in the same manner, next pushing the needle down at D and up at E, until you've appliquéd the entire piece.

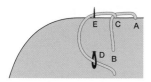

Blanket Stitch Diagram

assemble the petals

1. Randomly pair the red, green, yellow, and black print Pattern E pieces. Janet feels making the front and back pieces of petals different adds interest to a quilt.

2. Machine-stitch each pair together using a short stitch length and a ¼" seam allowance; leave the short straight ends open. Sew a second seam ⅛" outside of the first seam line.

3. Trim each pair close to the outside seam line, and turn right side out to make 112 petals; press.

4. Using two strands of embroidery floss, blanket-stitch around each petal, leaving the open ends unstitched.

add the borders

1. Cut and piece the green print 2×22" strips into the following:
- 2—2×33½" inner border strips
- 2—2×30½" inner border strips

2. Aligning raw edges, arrange 13 petals along each edge of the appliquéd quilt center, leaving a 1¾" space at each corner (see Petal Assembly Diagram, *below left*). Baste the petals in place.

3. Sew the short inner border strips to opposite edges of the quilt center. Then join the long inner border strips to the remaining edges of the quilt center. Press all seam allowances toward the inner border.

4. Aligning raw edges, arrange 15 petals along each edge of the inner border, leaving a 1¾" space at each corner. Baste the petals in place.

5. Sew the black print short outer border strips to opposite edges of the quilt center. Then join the black print long outer border strips to the remaining edges of the quilt center to complete the quilt top. Press all seam allowances toward the inner border.

complete the quilt

1. Layer the quilt top, batting, and backing according to the instructions in Quilting Basics, which begins on *page 94*. Quilt as desired.

2. Use the yellow print and green print 2½×22" strips to bind the quilt according to the instructions in Quilting Basics.

Starburst
Penny Rug
Pattern D

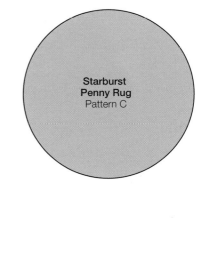

Starburst
Penny Rug
Pattern C

Starburst
Penny Rug
Pattern A

Starburst
Penny Rug
Pattern B

Full-Size Patterns

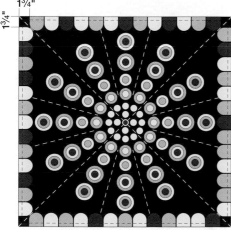

Petal Assembly Diagram

1¾"

1¾"

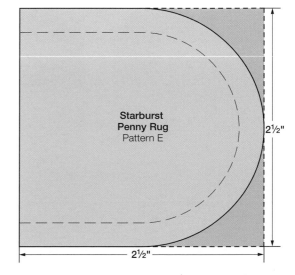

Starburst
Penny Rug
Pattern E

2½"

2½"

waving flag

Rich tones and a variety of fabrics bring a coordinated scrappy look to this quilt. For a simpler look, use just one beige print and one red print for the stripes.

Designer: Diane Hansen   Photographer: Scott Little

materials

- 10—2½×15" strips of assorted navy blue prints for flag
- 6—⅛-yard pieces of assorted red prints, stripes, and plaids for flag
- 5—⅛-yard pieces of assorted beige prints, stripes, and plaids for flag
- ¼ yard of black print for inner border
- ⅞ yard of brown print for outer border and binding
- Scraps of assorted brown prints and plaids for border
- 1—10×12" piece of gold plaid for large star appliqué
- 2—7" squares of gold prints for medium star appliqués
- 2—6" squares of gold prints and plaids for small star appliqués
- 4½×16" piece of blue print for USA appliqués
- 1½ yards of backing fabric
- 38×52" of quilt batting
- Freezer paper
- ¼ yard of lightweight fusible web

FINISHED QUILT TOP: 46×32"

Quantities specified for 44/45"-wide, 100% cotton fabrics. All measurements include a ¼" seam allowance. Sew with right sides together unless otherwise stated.

cut the fabrics

To make the best use of your fabrics, cut the pieces in the order that follows.

The patterns begin on *page 71*. To use freezer-paper templates for appliquéing, as was done in this project, complete the following steps.

1. Position the freezer paper, shiny side down, over the patterns. With a pencil, trace each pattern the number of times indicated. Cut out the freezer-paper templates on the traced lines.

2. Place a small amount of fabric glue on the matte side of the freezer-paper templates and anchor them onto the backs of the designated fabrics, leaving approximately ½" between templates for seam allowances. Cut out the fabric appliqué pieces about ¼" beyond the freezer-paper edges.

3. Use the point of a hot, dry iron to fold under and press the seam allowances onto the shiny side of the freezer-paper template. Clip curves as necessary.

From assorted navy blue prints, cut:
- 2—2½×14½" strips
- 2—2½×10½" strips
- 2—2½×8½" strips
- 2—2½×6½" strips
- 2—2½×4½" strips

From assorted red prints, stripes, and plaids, cut:
- 1—2½×20½" strip
- 1—2½×18½" strip
- 1—2½×16½" strip
- 2—2½×14½" strips
- 3—2½×12½" strips
- 1—2½×10½" strip
- 23—2⅞" squares, cutting each diagonally in half to make 46 triangles

From assorted beige prints, stripes, and plaids, cut:
- 1—2½×18½" strip
- 1—2½×16½" strip
- 2—2½×14½" strips
- 1—2½×12½" strip
- 2—2½×10½" strips
- 22—2⅞" squares, cutting each diagonally in half to make 44 triangles

From black print, cut:
- 2—1½×38½" inner border strips
- 2—1½×22½" inner border strips

From brown print, cut:
- 4—4½×42" strips for outer border
- 4—2½×42" binding strips

From assorted brown prints and plaids, cut:
- 8—2⅞" squares, cutting each diagonally in half to make 16 triangles

From gold plaid, cut:
- 1 of pattern A

From gold prints and plaids, cut:
- 2 *each* of patterns B and C

assemble the triangle-squares

1. Join two assorted red print, plaid, or stripe triangles to make a red triangle-square (see Diagram 1). Press the seam allowance toward the darker fabric. The pieced triangle-square should measure 2½" square, including the seam allowances. Repeat to make a total of 23 red triangle-squares.

Diagram 1

2. Referring to Diagram 2, repeat Step 1 using the assorted beige print, plaid, and stripe triangles to make a total of 22 beige triangle-squares.

Diagram 2

3. Repeat Step 1 using the assorted brown print and plaid triangles to make a total of eight brown triangle-squares (see Diagram 3).

Diagram 3

assemble the flag

1. Aligning long edges, sew together the two assorted navy blue print 2½×6½" strips. Then join an assorted navy blue print 2½×4½" strip to each short edge of the pieced strips (see Diagram 4). Press the seam allowances toward the outer strips.

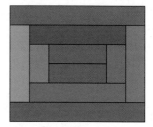

Diagram 4

2. Continuing to use Diagram 4 for reference, add the two assorted navy blue print 2½×10½" strips to the long edges of the pieced unit. Then add the two assorted navy

blue print 2½×8½" strips to the short edges. Add the two assorted navy blue print 2½×14½" strips to the long edges of the pieced unit to complete the flag's blue field; press. The pieced blue field should measure 12½×14½", including the seam allowances.

3. Referring to Diagram 5, *bottom left,* for placement, lay out the assorted red print 2½"-wide strips, the assorted beige print 2½"-wide strips, the red triangle-squares, and the beige triangle-squares in a short section and a long section. Sew together the pieces in each section. Join the pieced blue field to the short section. Then add the long section to make the pieced flag. The pieced flag should measure 22½×36½", including the seam allowances; press.

assemble and add the borders

1. Sew the short black print inner border strips to the side edges of the pieced flag. Then add the long black print inner border strips to the top and bottom edges of the pieced flag. Press the seam allowances toward the border.

2. Cut and piece the brown print 4½×42" strips to make the following:
- 1—4½×46½" outer border strip
- 2—4½×24½" outer border strips
- 2—4½×19½" outer border strips

3. Sew the brown print 4½×24½" outer border strips to the side edges of the pieced flag. Then add the brown print 4½×46½" outer border strip to the top edge of the pieced flag. Press the seam allowance toward the border.

4. Sew the eight brown triangle-squares into two horizontal rows (see Diagram 6, *below,* for placement). Sew together the rows and press. Sew a brown print 4½×19½" outer border strip to each edge of the brown triangle-square unit to make a pieced border unit; press. Add the pieced border unit to the bottom edge of the pieced flag to complete the quilt top. Press the seam allowance toward the outer border.

appliqué the stars

1. Referring to the photograph on *page 69* for placement, arrange the star appliqués on the pieced flag.

2. Use gold thread to appliqué the stars in place, leaving a ¼" opening along an edge in each. Using the openings for access, remove the templates by sliding your needle between the fabrics and freezer-paper templates. Gently loosen and pull out the freezer-paper templates. Stitch the openings closed.

Diagram 6

Diagram 5

appliqué the letters

1. Lay the fusible web, paper side up, over the letter patterns "U," "S," and "A." Use a pencil to trace each pattern once, leaving a ½" space between tracings. Cut out each piece roughly ¼" outside the traced lines.

2. Following the manufacturer's instructions, press the fusible-web shapes onto the wrong sides of the blue print 4½×16" rectangle; let cool. Cut out the fabric shapes on the drawn lines. Peel off the paper backings.

3. Referring to the photograph on *page 69*, arrange the letter appliqués on the quilt top; fuse in place.

4. Using blue thread, satin-stitch the appliqués in place.

complete the quilt

1. Layer the quilt top, batting, and backing according to the instructions in Quilting Basics, which begins on *page 94*. Quilt as desired.

2. Use the brown print 2½×42" strips to bind the quilt according to the instructions in Quilting Basics.

OPTIONAL DESIGN
Select fabrics in bright batik reds, whites, and blues, as our quilt tester Laura Boehnke did.

Waving Flag

Waving Flag

Full-Size Patterns

Full-Size Pattern

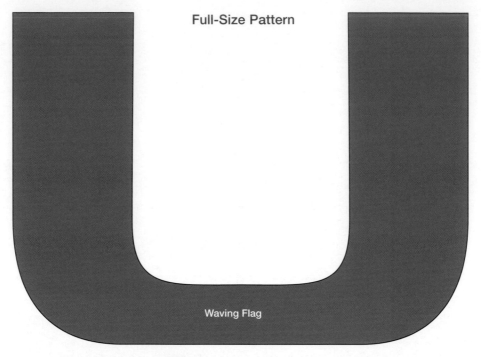

Waving Flag

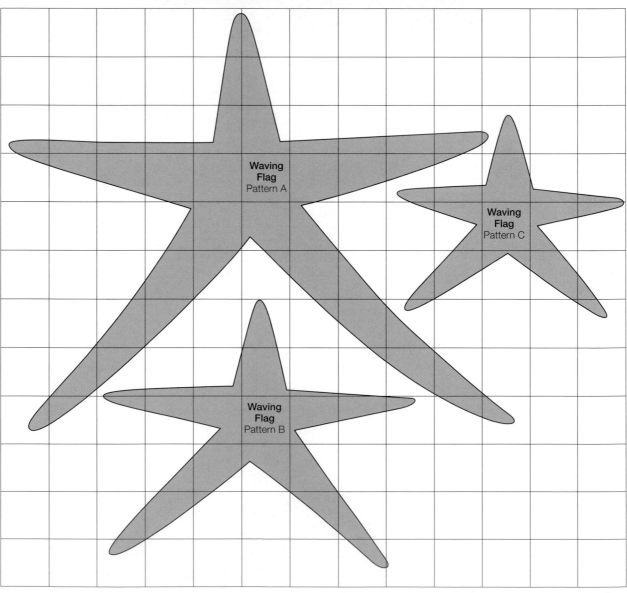

Waving
Flag
Pattern A

Waving
Flag
Pattern C

Waving
Flag
Pattern B

1 Square = 1 Inch

traditional
with a twist

This creative take
on traditional
appliqué combines
appliqué and
quilting into one
time-saving step.
Learn this unique
technique and
add a valuable
skill to your
appliqué repertoire.

heart
and hand

Put your hand-stitching skills to work with this quilt that utilizes a method of simultaneous quilting and appliquéing. When you're finished, you'll have the perfect gift for a special friend or relative.

Designer: Tonee White
Photographer: Perry Struse

materials

- 2¼ yards total of assorted plaids, stripes, dots, small prints, and solids in a variety of colors
- ½ yard of tan polka dot for binding
- 46" square of backing fabric
- 46" square of quilt batting
- Perle cotton No. 8 or embroidery floss in assorted colors
- 24—½"-diameter heart-shape buttons in red, green, and gold

FINISHED QUILT TOP: 39" square

Quantities specified for 44/45"-wide, 100% cotton fabrics. All measurements include a ¼" seam allowance. Sew with right sides together unless otherwise stated.

designer tips

Designer Tonee White tea-dyed the fabrics she used in her quilt shown *opposite*, which mellowed and enriched the colors. This allowed her great flexibility in fabric choices because the tea-dyeing unified the assortment.

To tea-dye your fabrics, prewash them. Fill a 4-gallon bucket half full of hot water. Add a 3-ounce jar of instant tea; stir to dissolve. Add prewashed fabrics. Soak at least 4 hours or overnight. Spread fabrics out in the sun to dry, leaving a wrinkle here and there to create interesting streaks.

Designer Tonee White's "appliquilt" technique involves layering a pieced quilt top with batting and backing, then appliquéing through all three layers. Using thread in a contrasting color gives the finished project a country look and disguises minor appliqué flaws, such as less-than-smooth curves.

The following instructions incorporate Tonee's technique. This quilt can also be constructed using your favorite appliqué method.

cut the fabrics

To make the best use of your fabrics, cut the pieces in the order that follows.

To make templates of the patterns, found on *page 77,* follow the instructions in Appliqué Primer, which begins on *page 84.* When cutting out the appliqué pieces, add a ³⁄₁₆" seam allowance.

From assorted plaids, stripes, dots, small prints, and solids, cut:
- 6—2×42" strips for checkerboard
- 4—8" squares for center applique foundations
- 4—6½" squares for corner applique foundations
- 28—3½×6½" rectangles for flower applique foundations
- 48—4¼" squares for Hourglass blocks
- 4 *each* of patterns B, D, and E
- 2 *each* of patterns A, A reversed, C, and C reversed
- 28 *each* of patterns G and H
- 16 of Pattern F
- 12 of Pattern F reversed

From tan polka dot, cut:
- 5—2½×42" binding strips

piece the quilt center

1. Lay out the four 8"-square center applique foundations in two rows of two squares each. Sew together the squares in each row. Press the seam allowances in opposite directions.

2. Then join the rows to make the quilt center. Press the seam allowances in one direction. The pieced quilt center should measure 15½" square.

cut and piece the checkerboard border

1. Sew together two assorted 2×42" strips along long edges to make a strip set (see Diagram 1). Press the seam allowance in one direction. Repeat to make a total of three strip sets.

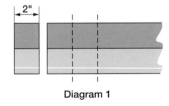

Diagram 1

2. Cut 2"-side segments from the three strip sets (see Diagram 1) to make a total of 48 segments.

3. Lay out 10 of the 2"-wide segments in a horizontal row (see Diagram 2, *above right*). Sew together to make a checkerboard border strip. Press the seam allowances in one direction. The pieced checkerboard border strip should measure 3½×15½", including

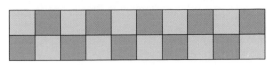

Diagram 2

the seam allowances. Repeat to make a second checkerboard border strip.

4. Sew the border strips to opposite edges of the pieced quilt center. Press the seam allowances toward the quilt center.

5. Lay out 14 of the 2"-wide segments in a vertical row. Sew together to make a side checkerboard border strip. Press the seam allowances in one direction. The pieced side checkerboard border strip should measure 3½×21½", including the seam allowances. Repeat to make a second side checkerboard border strip. Sew the border strips to the remaining edges of the quilt center. Press the seam allowances toward the quilt center.

assemble the flower border

1. Aligning long edges, sew together seven assorted 3½×6½" rectangles to make a flower border strip. Press the seam allowances in one direction. The pieced flower border strip should measure 6½×21½", including the seam allowances. Repeat to make a total of four flower border strips.

2. Sew the flower border strips to opposite edges of the pieced quilt center. Press the seam allowances toward the flower border.

3. Sew an assorted print 6½" square to each end of the remaining flower border strips to make flower border strip units. Press the seam allowances toward the 6½" squares. Sew the flower border strip units to the remaining edges of the quilt center. Press the seam allowances toward the flower border. The pieced quilt center should measure 33½" square.

assemble the hourglass border

1. Layer two contrasting 4¼" squares. Pair the remaining assorted 4¼" squares in the same manner.

2. For accurate sewing lines, use a quilter's pencil to mark a diagonal line on the wrong side of one square in each pair. (To prevent your fabric from stretching as you draw the lines, place 220-grit sandpaper under the paired squares.)

3. Stitch ¼" on each side of the drawn lines. To save time, Tonee suggests chain piecing machine-sewing the pairs together one after the other without lifting the presser foot or clipping threads between units (see Diagram 3). First, sew along one side of the drawn lines. Then turn the group around and sew along the other side of the lines. Clip the connecting threads between the squares.

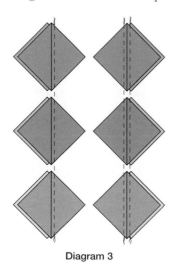

Diagram 3

4. Cut each pair of squares on the drawn line (see Diagram 4). Press the resulting triangle-squares open, pressing the seam allowance toward the darker fabric, to make a total of 48 triangle-squares.

Diagram 4

5. Layer two triangle-squares, matching the light triangles to the dark triangles (see Diagram 5). Pair the remaining triangle-squares in the same manner.

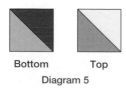

Bottom   Top

Diagram 5

6. Mark a diagonal line on the wrong side of one square in each pair (see Diagram 6).

Diagram 6

7. Stitch ¼" on each side of the drawn lines as before.

8. Cut each pair of squares on the drawn line. Press the resulting Hourglass blocks open, pressing the seam allowance in one direction, to make a total of 48 (see Diagram 7). Each Hourglass block should measure 3½" square, including the seam allowances.

Diagram 7

9. Sew together 11 Hourglass blocks, alternating the placement of the light and dark triangles, to make an Hourglass border strip. Press the seam allowances in one direction. The pieced Hourglass border strip should measure 3½×33½", including the seam allowances. Repeat to make a second Hourglass border strip.

10. Sew the Hourglass border strips to opposite edges of the pieced quilt center. Press the seam allowances toward the Hourglass border.

11. Sew together 13 Hourglass units to make a side Hourglass border strip. Press the seam allowances in one direction. The pieced Hourglass border strip should measure 3½×39½", including the seam allowances. Repeat to make a second side Hourglass border strip.

12. Sew the Hourglass border strips to the remaining edges of the quilt center to complete the quilt top. Press the seam allowances toward the Hourglass border. The pieced quilt top should measure 39½" square, including the seam allowances.

"appliquilt" the hands, hearts, and flowers

1. Layer the quilt top, batting, and backing according to the instructions in Quilting Basics, which begins on *page 94*. Tonee suggests machine-quilting in the ditch to secure the layers.

2. Pin the A and B pieces in place on the four center squares, referring to the photograph *below* for placement.

3. Knot the end of an 18" length of perle cotton. Starting underneath a heart ⅛" to ¼" inside the drawn line, bring the thread to the top of the heart, hiding the knot underneath the heart. Using the tip of your needle, fold under the seam allowance along the drawn line. Take the needle and thread down through the layers right next to the edge of the heart. The stitch will be perpendicular to the folded edge. This is simply a straight stitch through all layers. You are appliqueing and quilting in one step.

4. Continue stitching around the heart through all layers. Stitches should be ⅛" to ¼" apart.

5. In the same manner, "appliquilt" the remaining A and B pieces to the quilt. Then pin and "appliquilt" the remaining pieces to the quilt.

complete the quilt

Use the tan polka dot 2½×42" strips to bind the quilt according to the instructions in Quilting Basics. Add the 24 heart-shape buttons to the checkerboard border.

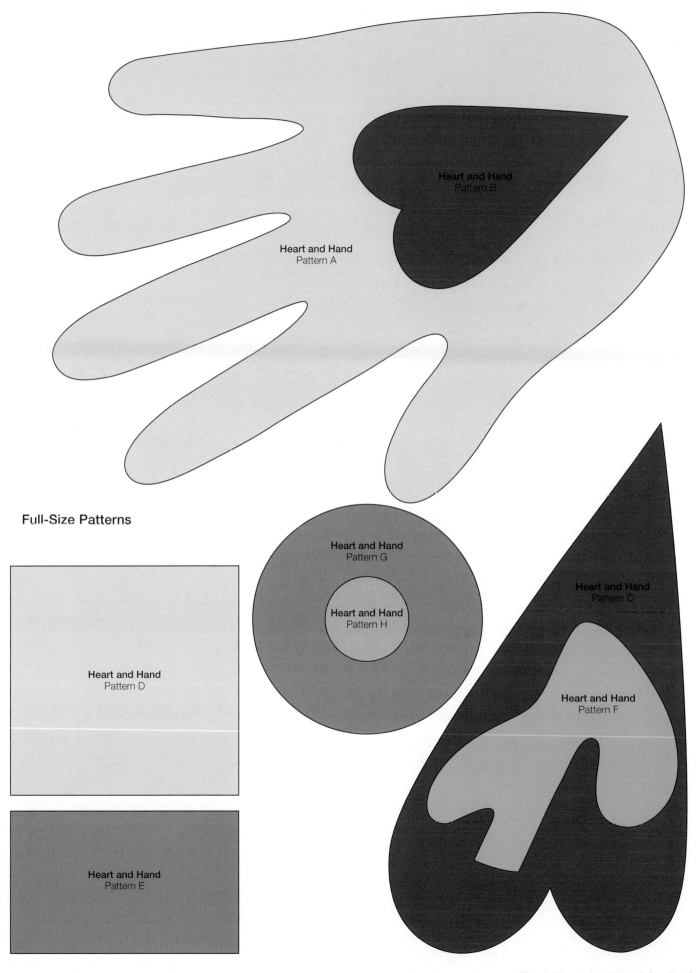

Full-Size Patterns

Heart and Hand
Pattern A

Heart and Hand
Pattern B

Heart and Hand
Pattern C

Heart and Hand
Pattern D

Heart and Hand
Pattern E

Heart and Hand
Pattern F

Heart and Hand
Pattern G

Heart and Hand
Pattern H

signs of
spring

Put a new spin on springtime with this fast and fun appliqué quilt. Combine the appliquéing and quilting into one simple step to create this "appliquilt" wall hanging.

Designer: Tonee White   Photographer: Scott LIttle

materials

½ yard of solid dark tan for appliqué
   foundation, blocks, and borders
¼ yard of dark lime green print
   for borders
½ yard of muslin for appliqué
   foundation
¼ yard of tan plaid for appliqué
   foundation
¼ yard of dark tan plaid for appliqué
   foundation
1—18×22" piece (fat quarter) of yellow-
   green print for appliqué
Scraps of assorted dark green, red, blue,
   tan, and gold prints for appliqués
5½×12½" piece of brown polka dot
   for basket appliqué
⅓ yard of dark gold print for binding
1 yard of backing fabric
36×41" of quilt batting
Embroidery floss: dark green, red, gold,
   blue, and black
21 assorted buttons

FINISHED QUILT TOP: 31×35½"

Quantities specified for 44/45"-wide,
100% cotton fabrics. All measurements
include a ¼" seam allowance. Sew with
right sides together unless otherwise
stated.

designer tips

Designer Tonee White's "appliquilt" technique
involves layering a pieced quilt top with
batting and backing, then appliquéing
through all three layers. Using thread in a
contrasting color gives the finished project a
country look and disguises minor appliqué
flaws, such as less-than-smooth curves.

The following instructions incorporate
Tonee's technique. This quilt can also be
constructed using your favorite appliqué
method.

cut the fabrics

To make the best use of your fabrics, cut the
pieces in the order that follows. The patterns
begin on *page 81*. To make templates from
the patterns, follow the instructions in
Appliqué Primer, which begins on *page 84*.
When cutting out appliqué pieces, add a ³⁄₁₆"
seam allowance.

From solid dark tan, cut:
- 1—21½×10½" rectangle for appliqué
  foundation
- 5—2¾" squares
- 13—1½×2½" rectangles

From dark lime green print, cut:
- 1—4½×36" rectangle
- 14—1½×2½" rectangles
- 5—2¾" squares

From muslin, cut:
- 1—15½×22½" rectangle for appliqué
  foundation

From tan plaid, cut:
- 1—6½×24" rectangle for appliqué
  foundation

From dark tan plaid, cut:
- 1—6½×34" rectangle for appliqué
  foundation

From yellow-green print, cut:
- Enough ¾"-wide bias strips to total 35" in
  length (For specific instructions on
  cutting bias strips, see Appliqué Primer.)

**From assorted dark green, red, blue,
tan, and gold prints, cut:**
- 1—1¼×30" strip for stem appliqué
- 1—1¼×20" strip for stem appliqué
- 31 of Pattern O
- 14 of Pattern Y
- 4 *each* of patterns A, A reversed, C,
  D, D reversed, E, and Q
- 3 *each* of patterns T, U, and V
- 2 *each* of patterns B, H, I, J, and P
- 1 *each* of patterns F, G, K, L, M, N,
  R, W, W reversed, and X

From brown polka dot, cut:
- 1 of Pattern S

From dark gold print, cut:
- 4—2¼×42" binding strips

assemble the hourglass border

1. Use a quilter's pencil to mark a diagonal
line on the wrong side of each solid dark tan
2¾" square. (To prevent your fabric from
stretching as you draw the lines, place 220-
grit sandpaper under the squares.)

2. Layer a marked solid dark tan 2¾" square atop a dark lime green print 2¾" square. Stitch ¼" away on each side of the drawn line. Cut on the drawn line and press open to create two triangle-squares (see Diagram 1). Press the seam allowances toward the solid dark tan triangles. Each triangle-square should measure 2⅜" square, including the seam allowances. Repeat to make a total of 10 triangle-squares.

Diagram 1

3. Cut each triangle-square in half perpendicular to the seam line (see Diagram 2) to make a total of 20 triangle subunits.

Diagram 2

4. Referring to Diagram 3, sew together two triangle subunits to make an hourglass unit. Press the seam allowances in one direction. The pieced hourglass unit should measure 2" square, including the seam allowances. Repeat to make a total of 10 hourglass units.

Diagram 3

5. Sew together the 10 hourglass units in a row to make the hourglass border. The pieced hourglass border should measure 2×15½", including the seam allowances.

assemble the rectangle border

1. Referring to the photograph on *page 79* and aligning long edges, lay out the 13 solid dark tan 1½×2½" rectangles and the 14 dark lime green print 1½×2½" rectangles, alternating the colors.

2. Sew together to make the rectangle border. Press the seam allowances toward the solid dark tan rectangles. The pieced rectangle border should measure 2½×27½".

assemble the quilt top

1. Referring to the photograph on *page 79*, sew the hourglass border to the top edge of the muslin 15½×22½" rectangle. Press the seam allowance toward the muslin rectangle.

2. Add the tan plaid 6½×24" rectangle to the right-hand edge of the muslin rectangle. Press the seam allowance toward the tan plaid rectangle.

3. Sew the solid dark tan 21½×10½" rectangle to the top edge of the pieced unit. Press the seam allowance toward the solid dark tan rectangle.

4. Join the dark tan plaid 6½×34" rectangle to the right-hand edge of the pieced unit. Press the seam allowance toward the dark tan plaid rectangle.

5. Sew the rectangle border to the bottom edge of the pieced unit. Press the seam allowance toward the muslin rectangle. Then add the dark lime green print 4½×36" rectangle to the left-hand edge to complete the quilt top. Press the seam allowance toward the dark lime green print rectangle.

prepare the quilt layers

1. Layer the quilt top, batting, and backing according to the instructions in Quilting Basics, which begins on *page 94*.

2. Quilt as desired. Tonee machine-quilted in the ditch between all pieces using monofilament or matching thread. Then she hand-quilted a 2"-wide diagonal grid in the solid dark tan 21×10½" rectangle, circles of various sizes in the dark lime green print 4½×36" rectangle, and 1"-wide parallel lines in the tan plaid 6½×24" rectangle and the dark tan plaid 6½×34" rectangle. She also hand-quilted a 3×5½" block grid in the muslin rectangle.

3. Use the dark gold print 2×42" strips to bind the quilt according to the instructions in Quilting Basics.

make the yo-yo flowers

1. Gather the assorted-color Y circles. Thread your needle with a color that matches a fabric; tie a heavy knot at the end. Use your fingers to fold under about ¼" for the hem.

Take running stitches (approximately four stitches per inch) all the way around the edge of the circle; do not cut your thread (see Diagram 4). Stitch just inside the fold line so the fabric will gather nicely.

Diagram 4

2. Pull the thread, gathering the edge to the center with the wrong side of the fabric inside (see Diagram 5), to make a small circle or yo-yo. Pull the thread tight; use your needle to knot it. Work the fabric and gathers to make the yo-yo lie flat. Press the yo-yo lightly. Repeat with the remaining fabric circles to make a total of 14 yo-yos.

Diagram 5

"appliquilting" the motifs

1. Referring to the photograph on *page 79* for placement, pin the appliqué pieces, including the yellow-green print bias strips and the prepared yo-yos, in place on the quilt top.

2. Knot the end of an 18" length of perle cotton thread. Starting underneath an appliqué piece and ¼" inside the appliqué line, bring your needle to the top, hiding the knot below the appliqué piece. Stitching through all layers and turning under the edges of the appliqué piece with your needle as you work, straight-stitch the appliqué piece to the quilt top. You'll be appliquéing and quilting in one step. Your stitches, perpendicular to the folded edge, should be ⅛" to ¼" apart. The stitches will resemble blanket stitching, although the thread won't run parallel to the appliqué.

3. In the same manner, stitch the remaining appliqué pieces, except for the assorted-color E circles, to the quilt top. Tack the yo-yos in place.

4. To make the "puffy" flowers, center and trace the dashed line on Pattern E onto the quilt top where you want your puffy flowers to be.

5. Pin the center of a fabric E circle to the center of a smaller drawn circle. Appliqué the fabric E circle to the quilt top on the drawn line, gathering slightly as you go.

6. Using a contrasting color of floss and a square knot, tack the fabric in a few places on top of the quilt. Clip the threads, leaving a short tail.

7. Repeat steps 5 and 6 for each puffy flower.

embellish the quilt

1. Using three strands of dark green embroidery floss, add straight stitches around the bases of the mushrooms for grass.

2. Using contrasting embroidery floss, add stitching details to the hearts and pears.

3. Tonee used a series of backstitches, lazy daisy stitches, and French knots to create flowers in the appliquéd flowerpots. (For specific instructions on backstitching, lazy daisy stitches, and French knots, see Embroidery Stitches on *page 93.*)

4. Add the 21 assorted buttons to the quilt top where desired.

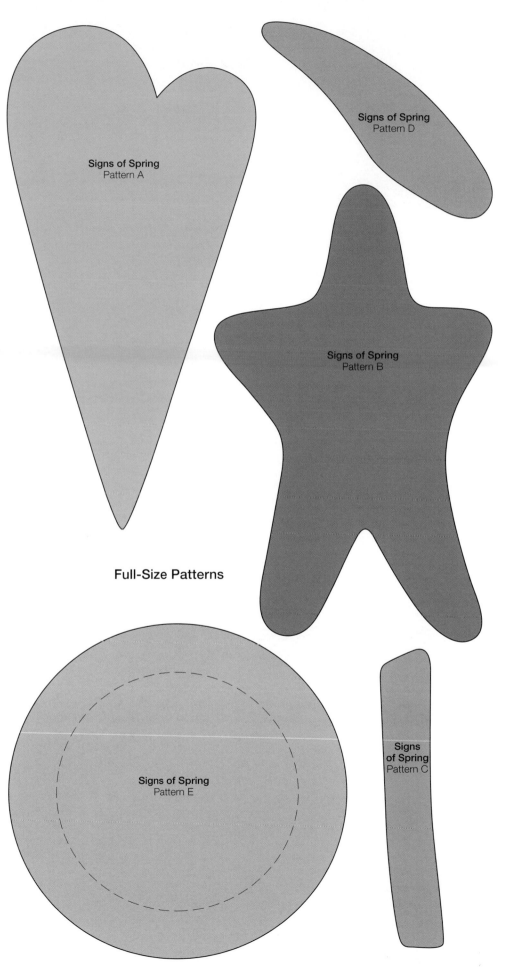

Full-Size Patterns

Signs of Spring
Pattern A

Signs of Spring
Pattern D

Signs of Spring
Pattern B

Signs of Spring
Pattern E

Signs of Spring
Pattern C

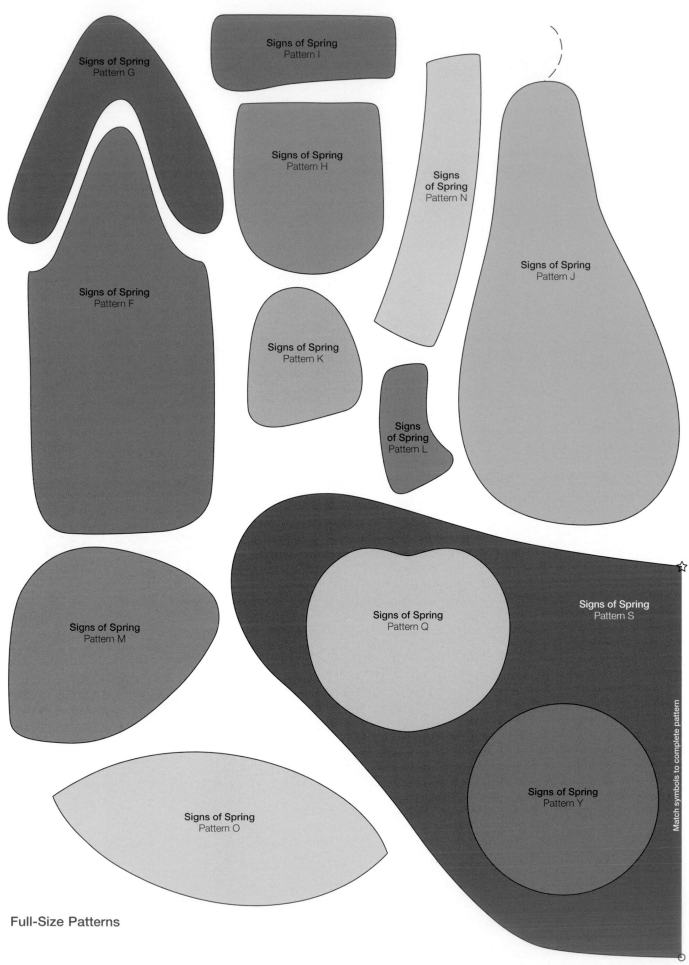

Signs of Spring
Pattern G

Signs of Spring
Pattern I

Signs of Spring
Pattern H

Signs
of Spring
Pattern N

Signs of Spring
Pattern J

Signs of Spring
Pattern F

Signs of Spring
Pattern K

Signs
of Spring
Pattern L

Signs of Spring
Pattern M

Signs of Spring
Pattern Q

Signs of Spring
Pattern S

Match symbols to complete pattern

Signs of Spring
Pattern Y

Signs of Spring
Pattern O

Full-Size Patterns

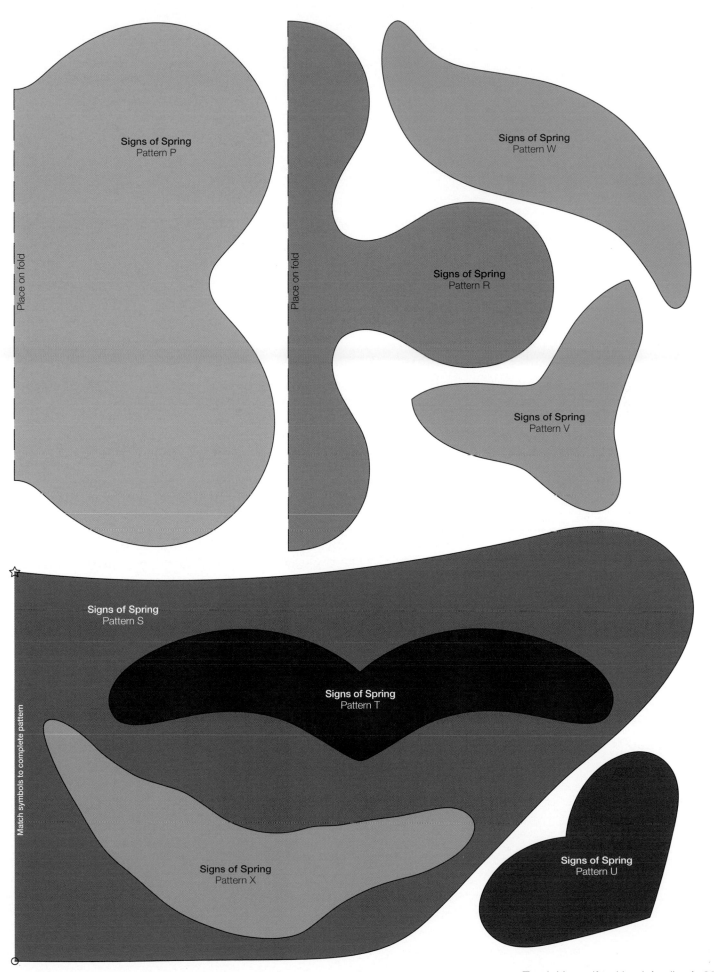

appliqué primer

The time-honored tradition of appliqué—adding fabric motifs to a foundation fabric—allows for freedom in design not always available with piecing. Styles range from simple to intricate, primitive to elegant. Appliqué can be done by hand or machine. Numerous appliqué methods have been developed, giving quiltmakers choices when it comes to the finished appearance.

templates

An appliqué template is a pattern used to trace the appliqué shape onto fabric. The template's material depends on how often the template will be used. Make sure that your template will hold up to the wear that it receives from multiple tracings without deteriorating at the edges. A sturdy, durable material such as template plastic, available at quilt and crafts supply stores, is suitable for making permanent templates for scissors-cut appliqué pieces.

making appliqué templates

1. For most appliqué techniques you need to make your templates the exact size of the finished pieces with no seam allowances included. The seam allowances are added when you cut out the appliqué pieces. Trace the patterns onto template plastic using a permanent marker. Use a ruler for any straight lines.

2. Mark each appliqué template with its letter designation, grain line (if indicated), block name, and appliqué sequence order. Mark an X on edges that do not need to be turned under and transfer the Xs to the fabric shapes when you trace around the templates.

3. Cut out each template, then verify their accuracy by placing them over their printed patterns.

using appliqué templates

1. Choose a marking tool to trace around the templates on fabric. A pencil works well on light-color fabric; a white, silver, or yellow dressmaker's pencil is a good choice on dark-color fabric. If you're using a pencil, keep the point sharp to ensure accuracy. Do not use a ballpoint or ink pen; it may bleed when washed. Test all marking tools on a fabric scrap before using them.

2. Place templates on the fabric, positioning them at least ½" apart. (Whether you place them faceup or facedown on the fabric's right or wrong side depends on the appliqué method you choose.) Trace around each template with your selected marking tool. The drawn lines represent the sewing lines. The specific appliqué technique you choose will dictate how much, if any, seam allowance you leave when cutting out the shape.

3. Cut out the appliqué shapes, including seam allowances if necessary for your chosen appliqué method.

stitching sequence

Edges of appliqué pieces that will be covered by other pieces do not need to be turned under before they are appliquéd. By preparing all your appliqué pieces at one time, you can plan any overlaps, which will save stitching time and considerable bulk in the finished project.

If your pattern does not indicate a numerical stitching sequence, observe which piece is closest to the foundation fabric and farthest away from you. That is the first piece you should appliqué to the foundation. Appliqué the rest of the pieces to the foundation, working from the bottom layer to the top.

preparing appliqué pieces

Prepare your appliqué pieces according to the needs of your chosen appliqué method. Preparation options include basting, freezer paper, double appliqué, and fusible web. Read the introduction to each method that follows to determine which one will work for your selected method.

basting method

This method uses a reusable template, marking tool, and thread to prepare appliqué pieces for hand or machine appliqué.

1. Place your templates on the right side of the fabric, positioning them at least ½" apart; trace.

2. Cut out the appliqué shapes, adding a ³⁄₁₆" seam allowance to all edges. Clip inside curves and points to within a thread of the marked lines, making clips closer together in the curved areas. Try to make your clips on the bias grain of the seam allowance, which means your clips will be often diagonal, rather than perpendicular, lines. This directional clipping prevents fabric from raveling while you're working with the edges. **Note:** Some hand quilters who use the needle-turn appliqué method choose to stop their appliqué preparation with this step.

3. Working from the right side of the appliqué piece and beginning at an inner point, use a contrasting color thread to baste the seam allowance under following the marked lines. For easier removal of the thread later, begin and end your basting thread on the right side of appliqué piece.

4. For a sharp outer point, fold the fabric straight over the point.

5. Fold in an adjacent seam allowance, overlapping the folded point. Baste in place.

6. As you reach the outer point, fold over the remaining adjacent seam allowance and continue basting around the shape.

using freezer paper

Many quilters choose to use freezer paper for appliqué. Available in grocery stores and some quilt shops, freezer paper has a shiny coating on one side that temporarily adheres to fabric when pressed with a warm iron. It is not necessary to consider the grain line of the fabric when utilizing freezer-paper templates.

freezer-paper method 1

This method uses freezer-paper templates to hold the seam allowances of the appliqué pieces in place. (Refer to Using Freezer Paper for additional information.) This technique may be used to prepare pieces for hand or machine appliqué.

1. Trace the appliqué patterns on the dull side of the freezer paper. Cut out the shapes on the traced lines to make freezer-paper templates.

2. Place the freezer-paper templates dull side up on the right side of the fabric. While holding the freezer paper in place, cut the shapes from fabric, adding a ³⁄₁₆" seam allowance to all edges.

3. Turn the freezer-paper templates shiny side up and place on the wrong sides of the appliqué shapes. Clip the inside curves or points on the appliqué shapes. When clipping inside curves, clip halfway through the seam allowances. Try to make your clips on the bias grain of the seam allowance, which means your clips often will be diagonal, rather than perpendicular, lines. This directional clipping prevents fabric from raveling while you're working with the edges.

4. Beginning at an inner point of an appliqué shape, use the tip of a hot, dry iron to push the seam allowance over the edge of the freezer paper. The seam allowance will adhere to the shiny side of the freezer paper. **Note:** Do not touch the iron soleplate to the freezer paper past the turned fabric edge.

5. Continue working around the appliqué shape, turning one small area at a time and pressing the seam allowance up and over the freezer paper. Make certain the appliqué fabric is pressed taut against the edges of the freezer-paper template.

Small pleats in the fabric may appear as you round outer curves. If there is too much bulk in a seam allowance, make small V clips around outer curves to ease the fabric around the edge.

6. For a sharp outer point, fold the fabric straight over the point of the freezer-paper template; press to freezer paper.

7. With the tip of the iron, push an adjacent seam allowance over the edge of the freezer paper. Repeat with the remaining adjacent seam allowance, pushing the seam allowance taut to ensure a sharp point.

8. After all edges are pressed, let the appliqué shape cool, then either remove the freezer-paper template before proceeding with the desired hand or machine-appliqué technique or leave in to stitch.

freezer-paper method 2

This technique involves pressing entire freezer-paper templates, shiny side down, to the appliqué fabric. The freezer paper is removed before the appliqué is sewn in place. This technique may be used to prepare pieces for hand or machine appliqué.

1. Trace a reverse image of the appliqué pattern on the dull side of the freezer paper. Cut out the shape on the traced lines to make a freezer-paper template. **Note:** To create a reverse image, tape the appliqué pattern facedown on a light box or sunny window.

2. Place the appliqué fabric wrong side up on a pressing surface. With a dry iron on the cotton setting, press a freezer-paper shape, shiny side down, to the appliqué fabric. Leave the iron on the paper for a few seconds. Lift the iron to check that the template is completely adhered to the fabric. If the template is not completely adhered, press again.

3. Cut out the appliqué shape, adding a 3/16" seam allowance to all edges. Clip inside curves or points on the appliqué shape. When clipping inside curves, clip halfway through the seam allowances. Try to make your clips on the bias grain of the seam allowance, which means clips often will be diagonal, rather than perpendicular, lines. This directional clipping prevents fabric from raveling while you're working with the edges.

4. Beginning at one inner point of an appliqué shape, use the tip of a hot, dry iron to push the seam allowance over the edge of the freezer paper. **Note:** The seam allowance will not adhere to the dull side of the freezer paper.

5. Continue working around the appliqué shape, turning one small area at a time and pressing the seam allowance up and over the freezer paper. Make certain the appliqué fabric is pressed taut against the edges of the freezer-paper template.

Small pleats in the fabric may appear as you round outer curves. If there is too much bulk in a seam allowance, make small V clips around outer curves to ease the fabric around the edge.

6. For a sharp outer point, fold the fabric straight over the point of the freezer-paper template; press.

7. With the tip of the iron, push an adjacent seam allowance over the edge of the freezer paper. Repeat with the remaining adjacent

seam allowance, pushing the seam allowance taut to ensure a sharp point.

8. After all edges are pressed, let the appliqué shape cool and then remove the freezer-paper template.

freezer-paper method 3

This technique involves pressing the shiny side of the freezer-paper templates to the right side of the appliqué fabric. The seam allowances are not turned under. (Refer to Using Freezer Paper on *page 85* for additional information.) This technique may be used to prepare pieces for needle-turn appliqué (see *page 91*).

1. Trace finished-size appliqué patterns onto the dull side of the freezer paper. Cut out the shapes on the traced lines to make freezer-paper templates.

2. Place the appliqué fabric right side up on a pressing surface. With a dry iron on the cotton setting, press a freezer-paper template, shiny side down, to the appliqué fabric. Leave the iron on the paper for a few seconds. Lift the iron to check that the template is completely adhered to the fabric. If the template is not completely adhered, press again.

3. Cut out the appliqué shape, adding a 3/16" seam allowance to all edges. Clip the inside curves or points on the appliqué shape. When clipping inside curves, clip halfway through the seam allowance. Try to make your clips on the bias grain of the seam allowance, which means your clips will be diagonal, rather than perpendicular, lines. This

directional clipping prevents fabric from raveling while you're working with the edges.

4. Do not remove the template until the appliqué piece is stitched in place.

double-appliqué method

This method eases the challenge of turning under seam allowances by facing the appliqué pieces with sheer, featherweight, nonfusible, nonwoven interfacing. This technique may be used to prepare pieces for hand or machine appliqué.

1. Place a rigid template wrong side up on the wrong side of the appliqué fabric; trace. The traced line is your stitching line.

2. With right sides together, layer your appliqué fabric with a like-size piece of sheer, featherweight, non-fusible, nonwoven interfacing.

3. Sew the pieces together, stitching on the marked line. Cut out the appliqué shape, adding a 3/16" seam allowance to all edges.

4. Trim the interfacing seam allowance slightly smaller than the appliqué fabric. This will enable the seam allowance to roll slightly to the back side of the appliqué once it is turned. Clip at the inner curves and points.

5. Clip a small slit in the center of the interfacing, being careful not to cut through the appliqué fabric.

6. Turn the appliqué right side out through the slit.

7. Press the appliqué piece from the right side.

fusible-web method

Manufacturer's instructions for adhering fusible web vary by brand. Follow the instructions that come with your fusible web to ensure success. Factors such as the iron's temperature setting, a dry or steam iron, and the length of time you press are critical to attaining a secure bond between the fusible web and the fabric.

This method eliminates the need to turn under any seam allowances. Choose a lightweight, paper-backed fusible web that can be stitched through unless you plan to leave the appliqué edges unfinished. This technique is commonly used for machine appliqué, but also can be used for hand appliqué.

1. Position the fusible web with the paper side up over the appliqué pattern and place on a light box.
Use a pencil to trace each pattern the specified number of times. If you are tracing multiple pieces at one time, leave at least 1/2" between tracings.

Note: If you are not using an appliqué pattern designed especially for fusible web, you will need to create a mirror image of the pattern before tracing it. If you don't, your appliqués will be reversed once you cut them from fabric. To create a reverse image, tape the appliqué pattern facedown on a light box or sunny window.

Cut out the traced appliqué pattern roughly 1/4" outside the traced lines. Do not cut directly on the traced lines.

2. If you are working with multiple appliqué layers or want to reduce the stiffness of the finished project, consider cutting away the center of your fusible web shapes. To do this, cut 1/4" inside the traced lines and discard the centers.

3. Place the fusible-web shape paper side up on the back of the designated appliqué fabric. Press in place following the manufacturer's instructions. Do not slide the iron, but pick it up to move it from one area to the next. Let the appliqué shape cool.

4. Cut out the fabric shape on the drawn lines. Peel off the paper backing.

making bias stems

Fabric strips needed to make curved appliqué stems and vines should be cut on the bias so that they are flexible enough to bend without wrinkles or puckers.

cutting bias strips

Strips for curved appliqué pattern pieces, such as meandering vines, and for binding curved edges should be cut on the bias, which runs at a 45° angle to the selvage of a woven fabric and has the most give or stretch.

To cut bias strips, begin with a fabric square or rectangle. Use a large acrylic ruler to square up the left edge of the fabric. Then make a cut at a 45° angle to the left edge (see Bias Strip Diagram). Handle the diagonal edges carefully to avoid distorting the bias. To cut a strip, measure the desired width parallel to the 45° cut edge; cut. Continue cutting enough strips to total the length needed.

Bias Strip Diagram

bias bar method

This method uses metal or heat-resistant plastic bias bars purchased in a size to match the desired finished width of the bias stem. If instructions for strip width and seam allowance are provided with your bias bars, refer to them. If not, refer to the following.

1. Cut a bias strip twice the desired finished width plus ¾". For example, for a ½"-wide finished bias stem, cut a 1¼"-wide bias strip. Handle the strip's edges carefully to prevent stretching. Fold the strip in half lengthwise with the wrong side together; lightly press.

2. Stitch the length of the strip with the folded edge on the machine seam guide (to the right of the presser foot), the raw edges to the left, and a seam allowance equivalent to the desired finished width. For example, for a ½"-wide finished bias stem, stitch ½" away from the folded edge.

3. Trim away the seam allowance, leaving only enough fabric to hold the seam intact (about ¹⁄₁₆").

4. Slide the bias bar into the stem with the seam allowance centered on a flat side of the bar. Press the seam allowance to one side so that neither the seam nor the seam allowance is visible along the edges.

5. Remove the bar from the stem, and press the stem again.

6. Trace the stem placement line on the appliqué foundation fabric as a seam guide.

7. Pin the bias stem to the appliqué foundation covering the marked line and secure the stem in place using a machine blind hem stitch or slip-stitching by hand.

finger-pressing method

1. Cut a bias strip to the desired finished width plus ½". For example, for a ¼"-wide finished bias stem, cut a ¾"-wide bias strip. Handle the strip's edges carefully to prevent stretching.

2. Finger-press under ¼" along both long edges.

3. Pin the bias stem to the appliqué foundation and secure the stem in place using a machine blind-hem stitch or slip-stitching by hand.

positioning the appliqué pieces

1. Cut the appliqué foundation fabric larger than the desired finished size to allow for any take-up in the fabric that might occur during the appliqué process. For example, for a 12" finished square, cut a 14"-square appliqué foundation. When the appliqué is complete, you'll trim the foundation to 12½" square. (The extra ¼" on each side will be used for seam allowances when assembling the quilt top.)

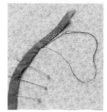

2. Fold the square appliqué foundation in half vertically and horizontally to find the center and then divide the square into quarters. Lightly finger-press to create positioning guides for the appliqué pieces.

3. Then fold the square appliqué foundation diagonally in both directions and lightly finger-press to make additional positioning guidelines.

4. Draw corresponding vertical, horizontal, and diagonal positioning guidelines on your full-size appliqué pattern if they are not already marked.

5. Prepare the appliqué pieces using the desired method. Referring to your appliqué pattern, pin and stitch the appliqué pieces to the foundation using your desired method; work from the bottom layer up.

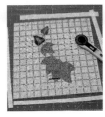

6. After the appliqué is complete, trim the appliqué foundation to the desired finished size plus seam allowances.

marked-foundation method

1. Cut the appliqué foundation fabric larger than the desired finished size to allow for any take-up in the fabric that might occur during the appliqué process. For example, for a 12" finished square, cut a 14"-square appliqué foundation. When the appliqué is complete, you'll trim the foundation square to 12½" square. (The extra ¼" on each side will be used for seam allowances when assembling the quilt top.)

2. Using a faint pencil line and your full-size appliqué pattern, trace the design onto the appliqué foundation fabric. To avoid having markings show after the appliqué is complete, lightly mark just inside the design lines and just at critical points (for example, where two lines intersect or at the tips of leaves).

3. Prepare the appliqué pieces using the desired method. (See Preparing Appliqué Pieces on *page 84*.) Referring to your appliqué pattern, pin and stitch the appliqué pieces to the foundation using your desired method; work from the bottom layer up.

4. After the appliqué is complete, trim the appliqué foundation to the desired size plus seam allowances.

light-box method

1. Cut the appliqué foundation fabric larger than the desired finished size to allow for any take-up in the fabric that might occur during the appliqué process. For example, for a 12" finished square, cut a 14"-square appliqué foundation. When the appliqué is complete, you'll trim the foundation square to 12½" square. (The extra ¼" on each side will be used for seam allowances when assembling the quilt top.)

2. Place your full-size appliqué pattern on a light box and secure it with tape. Center the appliqué foundation fabric atop the appliqué pattern.

3. Prepare the appliqué pieces using the desired method. (See Preparing Appliqué Pieces on *page 84*.) Return to the light box and pin the bottom layer of appliqué pieces in place on the appliqué foundation. Stitch the appliqué pieces to the foundation using your desired method.

4. After stitching the bottom layer of the appliqué pieces, return the appliqué foundation to the light box. Match the next layer of appliqué pieces with the pattern, pin, and stitch. Continue in this manner until all appliqué pieces are stitched to the foundation.

5. Trim the appliqué foundation to the desired size plus seam allowances.

overlay method

1. Cut the appliqué foundation fabric larger than the desired finished size to allow for any take-up in the fabric that might occur during the appliqué process. For example, for a 12" finished square, cut a 14"-square appliqué foundation. When the appliqué is complete, you'll trim the foundation square to 12½" square. (The extra ¼" on each side will be used for seam allowances when assembling the quilt top.)

2. Position clear upholstery vinyl (or other clear flexible plastic) over your full-size appliqué pattern; trace the design with a permanent marker.

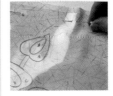

3. Center the vinyl overlay on the appliqué foundation fabric. Pin the top of the overlay to the foundation.

4. Prepare the appliqué pieces using the desired method. (See Preparing Appliqué Pieces on *page 84*.) Once the appliqué pieces have been prepared, slide the bottommost appliqué piece right side up between the appliqué foundation and the overlay. When the piece is in place beneath its corresponding position on the vinyl overlay, remove the overlay and pin the appliqué piece to the foundation. Stitch the appliqué to the foundation using your desired method.

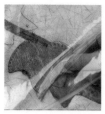

5. Pin the vinyl overlay on the foundation and position the next appliqué piece in the stitching sequence. Pin and stitch it to the foundation as before. Continue adding appliqué pieces in this manner until all appliqués have been stitched in place.

6. Trim the appliqué foundation to the desired size plus seam allowances.

holding appliqué pieces in place

Once the appliqués and foundations have been prepared for stitching, the appliqué pieces can be held in place with pins, basting threads, spray adhesive, fabric glue stick, or fusible web. The number of appliqué layers you're working with may influence your choice.

PINS: Use as many straight pins as needed to hold each appliqué piece in place on the appliqué foundation for both machine and hand appliqué. Pins are generally used to hold no more than two layers at a time and are pushed through from the top. Some hand appliquérs like to place pins on the back side of the work to prevent catching thread in pins as they work. Remove the pins as you stitch.

BASTING: Sewing long stitches about ¼" from the turned-under edges is another way to secure the prepared appliqué pieces to a foundation for both machine and hand appliqué. Begin and end the basting stitches on the right side of the appliqué for easier removal. You may wish to remove basting stitches when the entire appliqué work is complete or, if the basting threads impede stitching progress, remove

them as you go. This is the preferred method of quilters who wish to hold multiple appliqué layers in position at once before permanently stitching them in place.

FABRIC BASTING SPRAY: When lightly sprayed on the wrong side of appliqué pieces, this adhesive usually allows you to position and reposition the appliqués while you work. It can hold appliqués in place for both machine and hand appliqué. Work in a well-ventilated area and cover your work surface with paper. Be careful to spray lightly, as overspraying can cause a gummy build-up that makes stitching difficult.

FABRIC GLUE OR GLUE STICK: Apply these adhesives lightly to the wrong side of the prepared appliqué pieces along the outer edges or in the center. Press the appliqué piece to the appliqué foundation fabric. Be sure to apply the glue sparingly to avoid a build-up that would be difficult to stitch through. This method can be used for both machine and hand appliqué.

TIP: If residue from basting spray or a glue stick builds up on your needle, wipe it off with rubbing alcohol.

FUSIBLE WEB: This adhesive is most often used to hold pieces in position for machine appliqué, but it also can be used for hand appliqué. If you have an appliqué project with multiple layers of pieces that are prepared with fusible web, you may wish to hold them in position before adhering them to the foundation.

To do so, place your full-size appliqué pattern beneath a clear, nonstick pressing sheet. Layer the prepared appliqué pieces in position right side up on the pressing sheet. Press lightly, just enough to fuse the pieces together, following the manufacturer's instructions. Do not slide the iron, but pick

it up and move it from one area to the next. Let the pieces cool, then remove the fused appliqués from the pressing sheet and fuse them to the appliqué foundation.

hand appliqué

There are many ways to hand-stitch pieces in place on an appliqué foundation. If you're new to hand appliqué, experiment with each to determine which method is most comfortable for you.

For most hand appliqué, use a sharp, between, straw, or milliners needle and the finest thread you can find that matches the appliqué pieces. The higher the number, the finer the thread, so look for silk or fine cotton machine-embroidery threads; they will make your appliqué stitches nearly invisible.

traditional appliqué stitch

This technique uses appliqué pieces that have had the seam allowances turned under. For best results, use a sharp, between, straw, or milliners needle.

1. Prepare the appliqué pieces by turning the seam allowances under. Pin, baste, or glue an appliqué piece in place on the appliqué foundation.

2. Working with a length of thread no longer than 18", insert the needle into the wrong side of the appliqué foundation directly beneath the edge of the appliqué piece. Bring the needle up through the rolled edge of the appliqué piece.

TIP: If you're using appliqué pieces that have the freezer-paper template inside the appliqué shape while it's being stitched, be sure your stitching catches the fabric edge only. Keeping the paper template clear of stitching makes it easier to remove once the appliqué is stitched down.

 **3.** Hold the needle parallel to the edge of the appliqué with the point of the needle next to the spot where the thread just exited.

 **4.** Slide the point of the needle under the appliqué edge, into the appliqué foundation, and forward about ⅛" to ³⁄₁₆", bringing the needle point out through the rolled edge of the appliqué.

 **5.** Give the thread a gentle tug to bury the stitch in the fabric and allow the appliqué shape to rise up off the foundation. Continue stitching the same way all around the shape along the rolled edge.

TIP: Match your thread color to the appliqué pieces. *Note:* Contrasting thread was used in the photos for illustration purposes only.

 **6.** On the wrong side of the appliqué foundation, the stitches will be slightly angled.

 **7.** End the thread by knotting it on the wrong side of the foundation, beneath the appliqué piece.

8. Once all pieces have been appliquéd, press the foundation from the wrong side and trim it to the desired size, including the seam allowances.

TIP: Removing a freezer-paper template after an appliqué shape has been stitched in place can be done in a couple of different ways.

- You may stitch the appliquéd shape to the foundation, leaving a small opening to pull out the template. Use the tip of your needle to loosen the freezer-paper template. Pull the template out through the opening and stitch the opening closed.

- You may stitch the entire appliqué shape in place. From the wrong side, carefully snip through the appliqué foundation only. Remove the template through the opening, then stitch the opening closed.

needle-turn appliqué

This technique involves turning under the appliqué seam allowance as you stitch. For best results, use a straw or milliners needle. The extra length of these needles aids in tucking fabric under before taking stitches.

1. Prepare the appliqué pieces following Freezer-Paper Method 3 or by completing steps 1 and 2 of the Basting Method. Pin, baste, or glue an appliqué piece in place on the appliqué foundation.

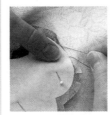 **2.** Working with a length of thread no longer than 18", insert the needle into the wrong side of the appliqué foundation directly beneath the edge of the appliqué piece. Bring your needle up between the appliqué and the foundation. Use the point of the needle to sweep the seam allowance under about 1" or so ahead of your stitching and secure the fabric with your thumb. The edge of the freezer-paper template or the drawn line serves as your guide for how much to turn under.

 **3.** Hold the needle parallel to the edge of the appliqué with the needle's point at the spot where the thread just exited. Slide the point of the needle under a thread or two along the appliqué's rolled edge. Give the thread a gentle tug to bury the stitch in the fabric and allow the appliqué shape to rise up off the foundation.

4. Then place the tip of the needle into the appliqué foundation and rock it forward, bringing the tip up into the rolled appliqué edge about ⅛" to ³⁄₁₆" away from the previous stitch. Pull the needle through and gently tug the thread to bury the stitch as before.

5. Continue in the same manner around the entire appliqué, taking tinier stitches around inside corners and curves where the seam allowances are more scant. Use the needle point to manipulate the seam allowance to lie flat in outside curves.

6. End the thread by knotting it on the wrong side of the foundation, beneath the appliqué piece.

7. Once all pieces have been appliquéd, press the foundation from the wrong side and trim it to the desired size, including the seam allowances.

wool appliqué

Felted wool—wool that has been napped and shrunk—is easy to work with because the edges will not ravel so there is no need to turn them under. Use templates to cut felted wool into appliqué pieces. Do not include seam allowances.

Use a basic running stitch or decorative hand-stitches to attach wool appliqués to an appliqué foundation. Or, for added dimension, tack wool appliqué pieces at their centers only.

To felt wool for use in appliqué, machine-wash it in a hot-water/cool-rinse cycle with a small amount of detergent, machine-dry, and steam-press. It is the disparity in temperatures, along with the agitation, that causes the wool to felt. If you wish to use wool from a piece of clothing, cut it apart and remove the seams so it can shrink freely.

tack stitch

This technique uses appliqué pieces that have had the seam allowances turned. (For more information, see Preparing Appliqué Pieces, which begins on *page 84.*) For best results, use a sharp, between, straw, or milliners needle.

1. Prepare the appliqué pieces by turning the seam allowances under. Pin, baste, or glue an appliqué piece in place on the appliqué foundation.

2. Working with a length of thread no longer than 18", insert the needle into the wrong side of the appliqué foundation directly beneath the edge of the appliqué piece. Bring the needle up through the rolled edge of the appliqué piece.

3. Insert the needle down into the foundation right next to the appliqué edge where it came up.

4. Bring the needle back up through the edge of the appliqué piece about $\frac{1}{16}$" from the first stitch. Continue in the same manner to stitch the appliqué piece to the foundation.

5. Once all pieces have been appliquéd, press the foundation from the wrong side and trim it to the desired size, including the seam allowances.

running stitch

This method results in a more primitive or folk art look. It uses appliqué pieces that have had the seam allowances turned under. (For more information, see Preparing Appliqué Pieces, which begins on *page 84.*) For best results, use a sharp, between, straw, or milliners needle.

1. Prepare the appliqué pieces by turning the seam allowances under. Pin, baste, or glue an appliqué piece in place on the appliqué foundation.

2. Working with a length of thread no longer than 18", insert the needle into the wrong side of the appliqué foundation directly beneath the edge of the appliqué piece. Bring the needle up through the appliqué piece about $\frac{1}{16}$" from the rolled edge.

3. Weave the needle in and out through both the edge of the appliqué piece and the foundation, staying about $\frac{1}{16}$" from the outside edge of the appliqué. Rock the needle in and out, taking small, evenly spaced stitches. Continue in this manner to secure the appliqué piece to the background.

4. Working with perle cotton and a larger needle, you can produce a larger running stitch, sometimes called a utility stitch or big stitch. The standard running stitch done in matching thread is shown *opposite*.

5. Once all pieces have been appliquéd, press the foundation from the wrong side and trim it to the desired size, including the seam allowances.

embroidery stitches

Give the appliqué shapes on your quilting projects the perfect finishing touch with any of these attractive—and often functional—hand-embroidered accents.

backstitch

To backstitch, pull your needle up at A (see diagram *below*). Insert it back into the fabric at B, and bring it up at C. Push your needle down again at D, and bring it up at E. Continue in the same manner.

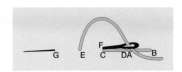

Backstitch

blanket stitch

To blanket-stitch, refer to the diagram *below*. First pull the needle up at A, form a reverse L shape with the floss, and hold the angle of the L shape in place with your thumb. Then push the needle down at B and come up at C to secure the stitch. Continue in the same manner, pushing the needle down at D and up at E, until you've gone completely around the piece.

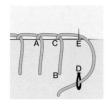

Blanket Stitch

french knot

To make a French knot (see diagram *below*), pull the thread through at the point where the knot is desired (A). Wrap the thread around the needle two or three times. Insert

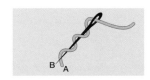

French Knot

the tip of the needle into the fabric at B, ¹⁄₁₆" away from A. Gently push the wraps down the needle to meet the fabric. Pull the needle and trailing thread through the fabric slowly and smoothly.

lazy daisy stitch

To make a lazy daisy stitch (see diagram *below*), pull the needle up at A and form a loop of thread on the fabric surface. Holding the loop in place, insert the needle back into the fabric at B, about ¹⁄₁₆" away from A. Bring the needle tip out at C and cross it over the trailing thread, keeping the thread as flat as possible. Gently pull the needle and trailing thread until the loop lies flat against the fabric. Push the needle through to the back at D to secure the loop in place.

Lazy Daisy Stitch

running stitch

To make a running stitch, pull your needle up at A (see diagram *below*) and insert it back into the fabric at B, ⅛" away from A. Pull your needle up at C, ⅛" from B, and continue in the same manner.

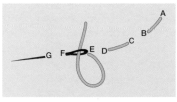

Running Stitch

satin stitch

To satin-stitch, see diagram *below*. Use a quilter's pencil to outline the area you want to cover. Then fill in the area with straight stitches, stitching from edge to edge and placing the stitches side by side.

Satin Stitch

straight stitch

To straight-stitch, pull your needle up at A (see diagram *below*) and insert it back into the fabric at B. Continue in the same manner.

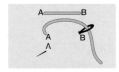

Straight Stitch

stem stitch

To stem-stitch, refer to the diagram *below*. First pull the needle up at A. Insert the needle into the fabric at B, about ⅜" away from A. Holding the thread out of the way, bring the needle back up at C and pull the thread through so it lies flat against the fabric. The distances between points A, B, and C should be equal. Pull with equal tautness after each stitch.

Stem Stitch

quilting basics

Read through these general quilting instructions to ensure you'll properly cut and assemble your quilt. Accuracy in each step guarantees a successful quiltmaking experience.

getting started

BASIC TOOLS

Acrylic ruler: To aid in making perfectly straight cuts with a rotary cutter, choose a ruler of thick, clear plastic. Many sizes are available. A 6×24" ruler marked in ¼" increments with 30°, 45°, and 60° angles is a good first purchase.

Rotary-cutting mat: A rotary cutter should always be used with a mat designed specifically for it. In addition to protecting the table, the mat helps keep the fabric from shifting while you cut. Often these mats are described as self-healing, meaning the blade does not leave slash marks or grooves in the surface, even after repeated usage.

Rotary cutter: The round blade of a rotary cutter will cut up to six layers of fabric at once. Because the blade is so sharp, be sure to purchase one with a safety guard and keep the guard over the blade when you're not cutting. The blade can be removed from the handle and replaced when it gets dull.

Scissors: You'll need one pair for cutting fabric and another for cutting paper and plastic.

Pencils and other marking tools: Marks made with special quilt markers are easy to remove after sewing.

Template plastic: This slightly frosted plastic comes in sheets about ¹⁄₁₆" thick.

Iron and ironing board: Pressing the seams ensures accurate piecing.

Sewing thread: Use 100% cotton thread.

Sewing machine: Any machine in good working order with well-adjusted tension will produce pucker-free patchwork seams.

HAND QUILTING

Frame or hoop: You'll get smaller, more even stitches if you stretch your quilt as you stitch. A frame supports the quilt's weight, ensures even tension, and frees both your hands for stitching. However, once set up, it cannot be disassembled until the quilting is complete. Quilting hoops are more portable and less expensive.

Quilting needles: A "between" or quilting needle is short with a small eye. Common sizes are 8, 9, and 10; size 8 is best for beginners.

Quilting thread: Quilting thread is stronger than sewing thread.

Thimble: This finger cover relieves the pressure required to push a needle through several layers of fabric and batting.

MACHINE QUILTING

Darning foot: You may find this tool, also called a hopper foot, in your sewing machine's accessory kit. If not, have the model and brand of your machine available when you go to purchase one. It is used for free-motion stitching.

Safety pins: They hold the layers together during quilting.

Table: Use a large work surface that's level with your machine bed.

Thread: Use 100% cotton quilting thread, cotton-wrapped polyester quilting thread, or fine nylon monofilament thread.

Walking foot: This sewing-machine accessory helps you keep long, straight quilting lines smooth and pucker-free.

CHOOSE YOUR FABRICS

It is no surprise that most quilters prefer 100% cotton fabrics for quiltmaking. Cotton fabric minimizes seam distortion, presses crisply, and is easy to quilt. Most patterns, including those in this book, specify quantities for 44/45"-wide fabrics unless otherwise noted. Our projects call for a little extra yardage in length to allow for minor errors and slight shrinkage.

PREPARE YOUR FABRICS

There are conflicting opinions about the need to prewash fabric. The debate is a modern one because most antique quilts were made with unwashed fabric. However, the dyes and sizing used today are unlike those used a century ago.

Prewashing fabric offers quilters certainty as its main advantage. Today's fabrics resist bleeding and shrinkage, but some of both can occur in some fabrics—an unpleasant prospect once you've assembled a quilt. Some quilters find prewashed fabric easier to quilt. If you choose to prewash your fabric, press it well before cutting.

Other quilters prefer the crispness of unwashed fabric, especially for machine piecing. And, if you use fabrics with the same fiber content throughout a quilt, then any shrinkage that occurs in its first washing should be uniform. Some quilters find this small amount of shrinkage desirable, because it gives a quilt a slightly puckered, antique look.

We recommend you prewash a scrap of each fabric to test it for shrinkage and bleeding. If you choose to prewash an entire fabric piece, unfold it to a single layer. Wash it in warm water to allow the fabric to shrink and/or bleed. If the fabric bleeds, rinse it until the water runs clear. Do not use it in a quilt if it hasn't stopped bleeding. Hang the fabric to dry, or tumble it in the dryer until slightly damp; press well.

finishing
LAYERING

Cut and piece the backing fabric to measure at least 3" longer on all sides than the quilt top. Press all seam allowances open. With wrong sides together, layer the quilt top and backing fabric with the batting in between; baste. Quilt as desired.

BINDING

The binding for most quilts is cut on the straight grain of the fabric. If your quilt has curved edges, cut the strips on the bias (see Appliqué Primer, which begins on *page 84*). The cutting instructions for projects in this book specify the number of binding strips or a total length needed to finish the quilt. The instructions also specify enough width for a French-fold, or double-layer, binding because it's easier to apply and adds durability.

Join the strips with diagonal seams to make one continuous binding strip (see Diagram 1, *above*). Trim the excess fabric, leaving ¼" seam allowances. Press seam allowances open. Then, with the wrong sides together, fold under 1" at one end of the binding strip (see Diagram 2, *above*); press. Fold the strip in half lengthwise (see Diagram 3, *above*); press.

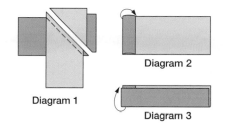

Diagram 1

Diagram 2

Diagram 3

Beginning in the center of one side, place the binding strip against the right side of the quilt top, aligning the binding strip's raw edges with the quilt top's raw edge (see Diagram 4, *right*). Beginning 1½" from the folded edge, sew through all layers, stopping ¼" from the corner. Backstitch, then clip the threads. Remove the quilt from under the sewing-machine presser foot.

Fold the binding strip upward (see Diagram 5, *right*), creating a diagonal fold, and finger-press.

Holding the diagonal fold in place with your finger, bring the binding strip down in line with the next edge, making a horizontal fold that aligns with the first edge of the quilt (see Diagram 6, *right*).

Start sewing again at the top of the horizontal fold, stitching through all layers. Sew around the quilt, turning each corner in the same manner.

When you return to the starting point, lap the binding strip inside the beginning fold (see Diagram 7, *right*). Finish sewing to the starting point (see Diagram 8, *right*). Trim the batting and backing fabric even with the quilt top edges.

Turn the binding over the edge of the quilt to the back. Hand-stitch the binding to the backing fabric, making sure to cover any machine stitching.

To make mitered corners on the back, hand-stitch the binding up to a corner; fold a miter in the binding. Take a stitch or two in the fold to secure it. Then stitch the binding in place up to the next corner. Finish each corner in the same manner.

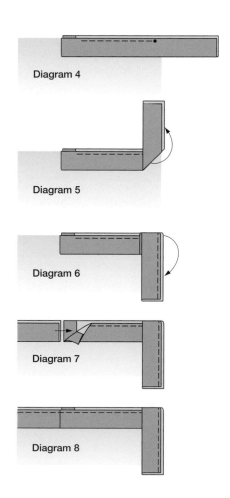

Diagram 4

Diagram 5

Diagram 6

Diagram 7

Diagram 8

Better Homes and Gardens®
Creative Collection™

Editorial Director
Gayle Goodson Butler

Editor-in-Chief
Beverly Rivers

Executive Editor Karman Wittry Hotchkiss

Art Director   **Contributing Editorial Manager**
Brenda Drake Lesch   Heidi Palkovic

Contributing Design Director Tracy S. DeVenney
Copy Chief Mary Heaton
Contributing Copy Editor Lisa Flyr
Proofreader Dana Schmidt
Administrative Assistant Lori Eggers

Senior Vice President
Bob Mate

Publishing Group President
Jack Griffin

Chairman and CEO William T. Kerr
President and COO Stephen M. Lacy

In Memoriam
E. T. Meredith III (1933–2003)
